The Beginner's Guide to Drawing
Cartoons

A step-by-step guide to drawing fantastic cartoons

Paul B. Davies • Kevin Faerber
Terry Longhurst • David Pattison

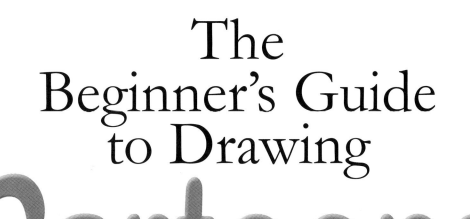

Text by Amanda O'Neill

p

This is a Parragon Publishing Book
This edition published in 2004

Parragon Publishing
Queen Street House
4 Queen Street
Bath BA1 1HE, UK

Copyright © Parragon 2003

Designed by Paul Turner and Sue Pressley
Cover design by Sarah Lever
Edited by Philip de Ste. Croix

ISBN 1-40540-543-0

Printed in China

About This Book

Cartoons are drawings which take a humorous look at the world. They are fun to look at, and they are fun to draw. This book shows you how to create a host of entertaining characters, building up your drawings in easy stages.

The tools you need are simple — paper, a selection of pencils, and an eraser. Fairly thick paper is best to work with (very thin paper wears through if you have to rub out a line).

To color in your drawings, you can use paints, crayons, colored inks, or felt-tip pens. Fine felt-tips are useful for drawing outlines, while thick ones are better for coloring in.

Remember that cartoons aren't meant to be realistic. They are imaginative and exaggerated. You can draw monsters or fairies, create cute animals or fearsome dinosaurs, or even give a cartoon character a nose that is bigger than his feet. Anything is possible in cartoon-land.

But they are meant to be recognizable. You need to get inside your subject just as much as if you were making an accurate portrait. Most cartoons take some feature of the subject and exaggerate it to comic effect. So you need to decide which feature you want to emphasize. It may be the way your subject stands, or moves. It may be big feet or a funny expression.

The step-by-step drawings in this book will give you plenty of ideas to get you started. After that, there's a whole world out there to draw!

Happy Fish

Fish come in many different shapes — long and thin, like eels, or short and rounded. But their bodies are always made up of curves. By exaggerating these natural curves, you can make your fish comically fat and cheerful-looking.

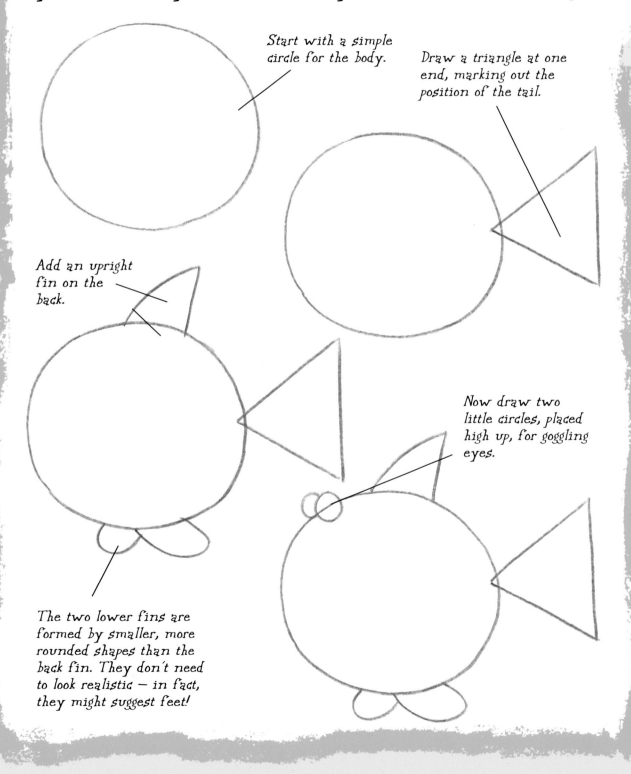

Start with a simple circle for the body.

Draw a triangle at one end, marking out the position of the tail.

Add an upright fin on the back.

Now draw two little circles, placed high up, for goggling eyes.

The two lower fins are formed by smaller, more rounded shapes than the back fin. They don't need to look realistic — in fact, they might suggest feet!

Sketch in a big happy smile. It curves beyond the edge of your circle to form a bulging lower lip. At the inside edge of the mouth, a small crescent shape forms a smiley dimple.

Now you can start inking in your details. Draw the tail within its guideline triangle, and shape the other fins with curvy lines.

You don't need to draw in all the scales — but you can suggest them with a few bold wavy lines. A line of bubbles gives a fun effect.

A little shading on the fins, tail and scales adds the final touch. Show your finished drawing to your friends, and they'll think you're fishing for compliments!

Sleepy Cat

Cats take sleeping very seriously. They invented the catnap, and spend two-thirds of their lives practicing it. When awake, cats have long, elegant, flowing lines — but a sleepy cat curls itself into a short, round shape like a fur hat.

Start with two overlapping egg shapes, one big and one small. The bigger 'egg', which forms the body, should be more than twice the size of the smaller one, which forms the head.

Add two pointed ears. Keep the right ear inside the body outline, so it does not break up the curve of the back.

An oval slightly above the center of the head forms a big, blobby nose.

The forelegs follow the curve of the chin, forming a rounded pillow under the head. Draw most of the tail just inside the line of the body, taking only the base and tip outside your original shape.

Two simple curves create a pair of eyes closed in sleep. When you draw in the hind leg, use a generous sweeping line so that the leg takes up about half the body space.

To finish the face, draw in big fat cheeks curving from just below the top of the nose. Make the outer edges jagged, to suggest fur, and add little dots for the whisker roots.

Ink in your lines, and add bold coat markings. Real cats have complicated fur patterns, but cartoon cats look better if you simplify these into a regular, eye-catching design.

The whole drawing is made up of curves, giving a rounded, comfortable effect. Paws folded into a pillow under his chin, the sleepy cat is a picture of comfort — snug and smug.

Smiley Snail

As most people know, a snail is only a slug with a mobile home! Most people find slugs rather unlovable, but the addition of a shell gives the snail a certain charm — unless you're a gardener. It also makes him more interesting to draw than his slimy cousin.

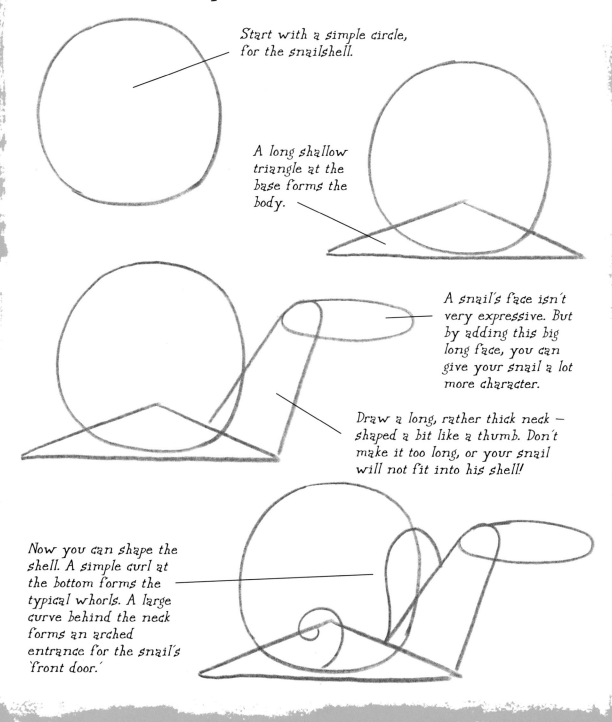

Start with a simple circle, for the snailshell.

A long shallow triangle at the base forms the body.

A snail's face isn't very expressive. But by adding this big long face, you can give your snail a lot more character.

Draw a long, rather thick neck — shaped a bit like a thumb. Don't make it too long, or your snail will not fit into his shell!

Now you can shape the shell. A simple curl at the bottom forms the typical whorls. A large curve behind the neck forms an arched entrance for the snail's 'front door.'

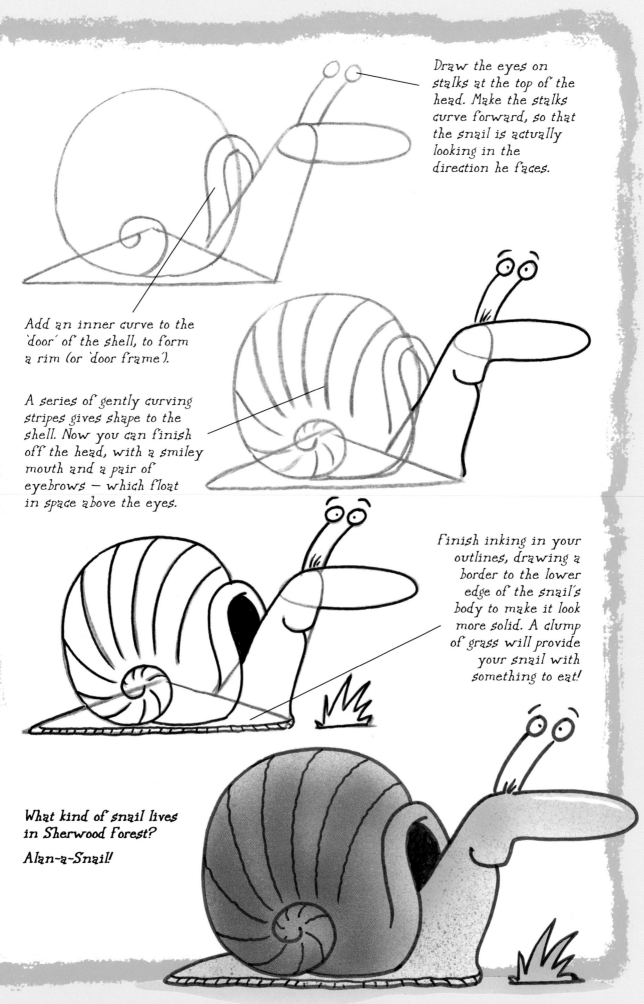

Draw the eyes on stalks at the top of the head. Make the stalks curve forward, so that the snail is actually looking in the direction he faces.

Add an inner curve to the 'door' of the shell, to form a rim (or 'door frame').

A series of gently curving stripes gives shape to the shell. Now you can finish off the head, with a smiley mouth and a pair of eyebrows — which float in space above the eyes.

Finish inking in your outlines, drawing a border to the lower edge of the snail's body to make it look more solid. A clump of grass will provide your snail with something to eat!

What kind of snail lives in Sherwood Forest?

Alan-a-Snail!

Chunky Chicken

Chickens are comical figures even in real life. Their chunky bodies balance between ridiculously small heads and legs. They are the busybodies of the farmyard, bustling about importantly and peering around with little bright eyes.

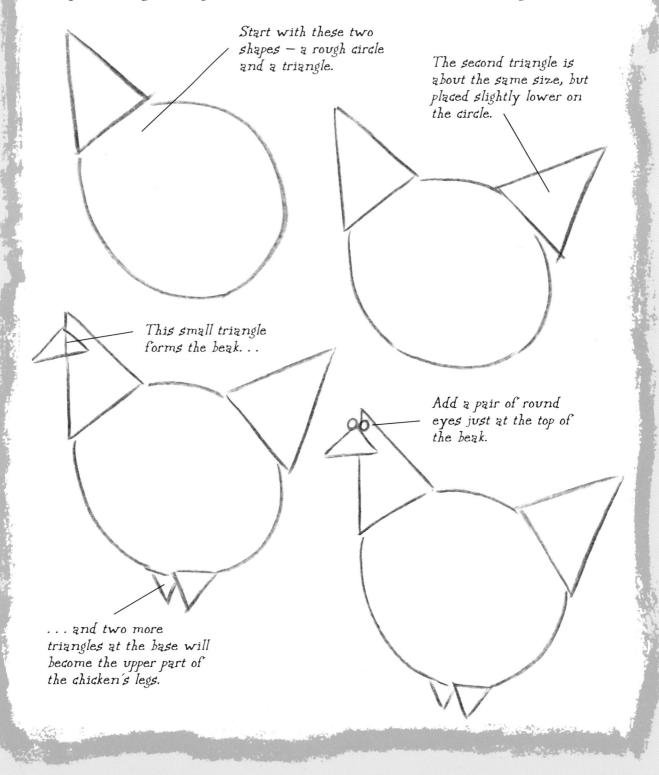

Start with these two shapes — a rough circle and a triangle.

The second triangle is about the same size, but placed slightly lower on the circle.

This small triangle forms the beak. . .

Add a pair of round eyes just at the top of the beak.

. . . and two more triangles at the base will become the upper part of the chicken's legs.

Draw a comb on top of the head, and two small wattles under the beak.

Add pupils to the eyes, draw in a wing and shape the tail feathers. Give a gentle curve to the neck and tail to form the ends of the dumpy, boat-shaped body.

Ink in your outlines and sketch in a few feathers on the wing and breast.

Now you can add the lower legs and long, flat feet.

Everyone knows the joke, 'Why did the chicken cross the road?' But do you know what to call a person who tells chicken jokes?

A comedihen!

Spike the Hedgehog

When is a hog not a hog? When it's a hedgehog! The only piggy thing about this little ball of spikes is the way he snorts and snuffles over his food. With a hundred spines per square inch, he is one of the prickliest characters you will ever meet.

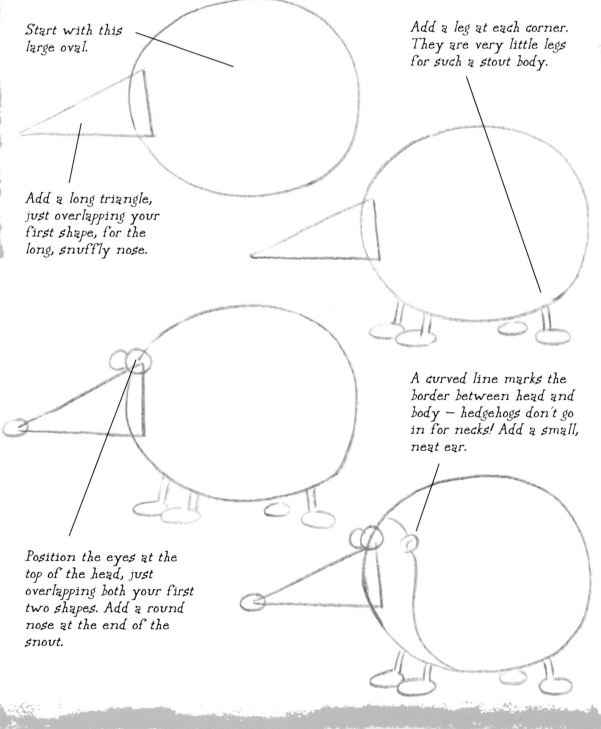

Start with this large oval.

Add a long triangle, just overlapping your first shape, for the long, snuffly nose.

Add a leg at each corner. They are very little legs for such a stout body.

A curved line marks the border between head and body — hedgehogs don't go in for necks! Add a small, neat ear.

Position the eyes at the top of the head, just overlapping both your first two shapes. Add a round nose at the end of the snout.

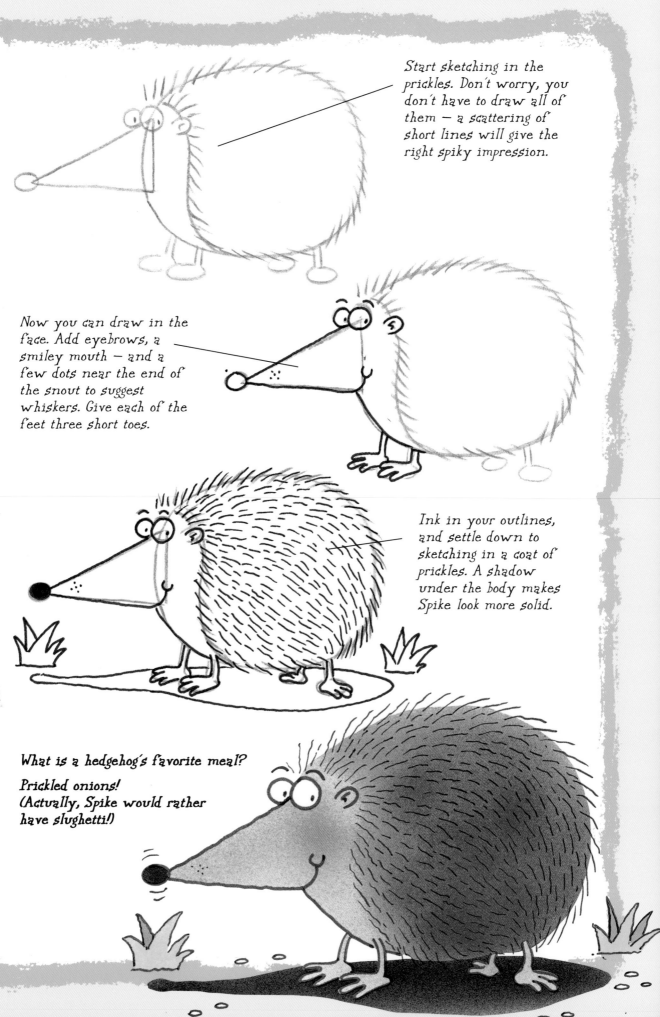

Start sketching in the prickles. Don't worry, you don't have to draw all of them — a scattering of short lines will give the right spiky impression.

Now you can draw in the face. Add eyebrows, a smiley mouth — and a few dots near the end of the snout to suggest whiskers. Give each of the feet three short toes.

Ink in your outlines, and settle down to sketching in a coat of prickles. A shadow under the body makes Spike look more solid.

What is a hedgehog's favorite meal?

Prickled onions!
(Actually, Spike would rather have slughetti!)

Hungry Mouse

Mice are among the most popular of cartoon characters. Mickey Mouse, Speedy Gonzales, Dangermouse, Topo Gigio, and Jerry (of Tom and Jerry fame) are just a few mouse favorites.

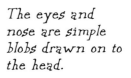

Add a pair of great big feet, a second ear — and a large square of cheese.

Start with these three shapes — rather like a bunch of balloons.

The eyes and nose are simple blobs drawn on to the head.

Add a bulge at the back to make a fat bottom. The final shape of the body will be more pear-shaped than oval. Don't forget the tail!

Draw in the arms and simple hands. One hand, naturally, reaches toward that tempting lump of cheese.

It's a dark night, and you can't get to sleep because you can hear a mouse squeaking in your bedroom. What should you do?

Oil it!

Draw some holes in the cheese to make it look more interesting.

Finish the details of the head — whiskers, buck teeth, and a little fringe above the eyes.

Now you can ink in your outlines, adding shadows under the mouse and his feast. Yummy!

What do you get when you cross a mouse with an elephant?

Huge holes in the skirting-boards.

Butch the Dog

Dogs come in a greater variety of shapes and sizes than any other kind of animal. With cartoon dogs, the range is even wider! You can draw a dog as cute as the heroine of *Lady and the Tramp*, or as butch as the feller below.

Start with a long oval, add a peak on top, and take down two curving shoulders rather like a cape.

Add these two big tear-shapes for ears. They don't have to be attached to the head!

Add two small circles for beady eyes.

Make the arms thin and bendy like pipe-cleaners for a comic contrast with the big body.

Now give him a big bone to gloat over, and a thick collar.

Between the nose and the collar, draw in a wide smile, with the tongue hanging out at the thought of that juicy bone.

Finish drawing the details of the head, with a tuft of fur on top.

Ink or paint the ears and nose black, leaving a white highlight on each to make them look rounded and shiny.

Why is it hard to find a dog going cheap?

Because they usually go woof!

Give your dog a firm grip on his bone by curving his 'fingers' around the ends.

Merry Reindeer

It's impossible to think of reindeer without thinking of Christmas and red-nosed Rudolph. But they do more than pull Santa's sleigh. In the frozen north where they live, they also pull buses, mail vehicles, and even army gear.

Start with a big triangle crossed by a large oval which will become your reindeer's nose.

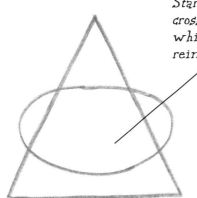

Now you have the basis of the head and that great big nose.

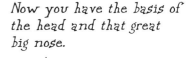

Add a skinny neck (yes, it does look a bit like a Christmas tree now!) and a circle at the base which will form a collar.

These two circles will make the eyes.

Two large, leaf-shaped ears are drawn from the edges of the eyes. Finish sketching in a collar at the base of the neck.

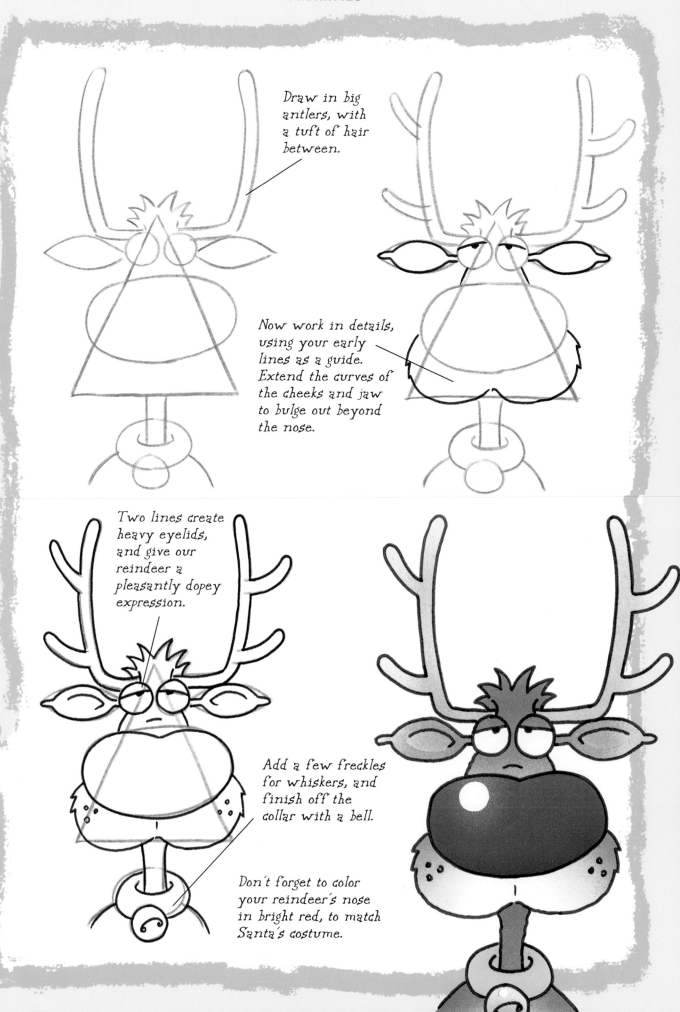

Draw in big antlers, with a tuft of hair between.

Now work in details, using your early lines as a guide. Extend the curves of the cheeks and jaw to bulge out beyond the nose.

Two lines create heavy eyelids, and give our reindeer a pleasantly dopey expression.

Add a few freckles for whiskers, and finish off the collar with a bell.

Don't forget to color your reindeer's nose in bright red, to match Santa's costume.

Gymnast

When you watch gymnasts in action, they move with grace and confidence. The humor in this cartoon comes from the absence of those very qualities. This gymnast looks like he's having real trouble clearing the vaulting horse.

Be careful how you space these ovals for the feet.

Start with an egg shape for the head, and this second shape for the shoulders and chest.

Adding hair and ears turns the 'egg' into a recognizable head.

Slightly curved arms reach down to grip the top of the vaulting horse.

Finish drawing the vaulting horse, and link the feet to the body with chubby legs.

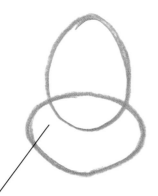

Draw in legs on the shorts and shoes.

A simple line for the mouth can still be very expressive.

Keep clothes simple. Short curved lines help to suggest the shape of the body inside.

Hands and feet don't need to be drawn in any great detail.

Draw your outlines slightly thicker under chin, legs of shorts, chest, etc. to suggest shadows.

Tennis Player

Some people play sports for fun. Others play to win! You can see which kind this tennis player is! But only half the story is told by his expression of manic determination. His tense, twisted posture is just as important.

The egg-shaped head is tilted one way, looking toward the ball. . .

Make the two shapes for the outstretched thighs slightly different in size and form. This one is shorter, because this leg faces toward us a little more.

. . . while the longer oval for the body tilts more strongly in the other direction.

Draw an oval for the tennis racket, slanting it at an angle. Make it nearly as big as the player's head.

This shape is the start of an outstretched arm.

The large feet, tucked under the body, are roughly bean-shaped. Be careful with your spacing, leaving room to fit in the calves of his legs.

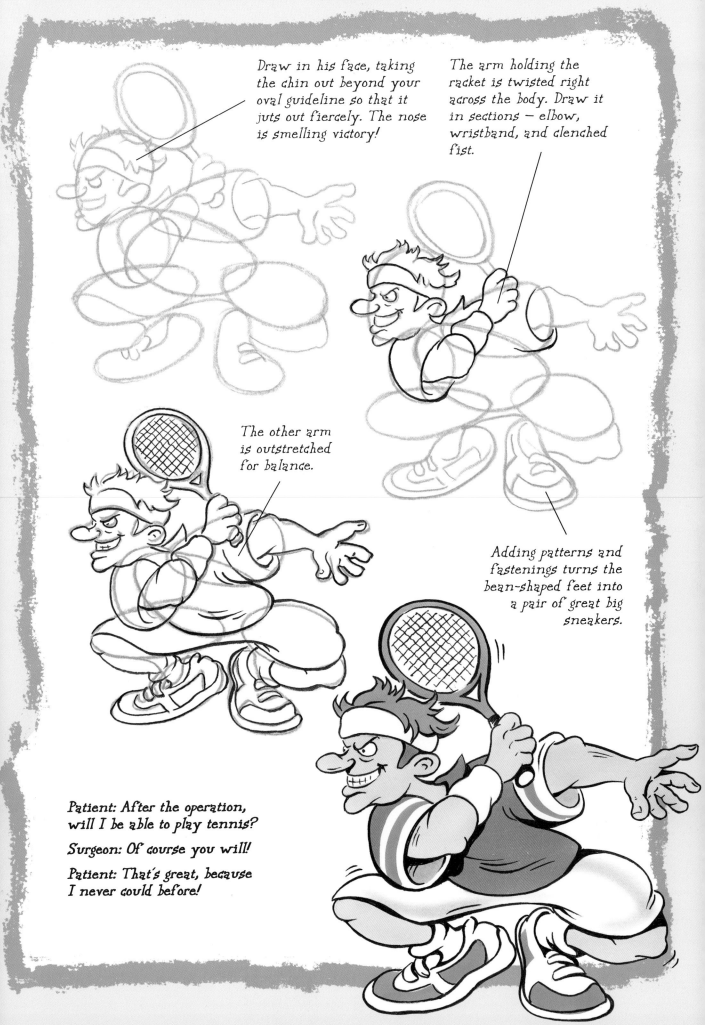

Draw in his face, taking the chin out beyond your oval guideline so that it juts out fiercely. The nose is smelling victory!

The arm holding the racket is twisted right across the body. Draw it in sections — elbow, wristband, and clenched fist.

The other arm is outstretched for balance.

Adding patterns and fastenings turns the bean-shaped feet into a pair of great big sneakers.

Patient: After the operation, will I be able to play tennis?

Surgeon: Of course you will!

Patient: That's great, because I never could before!

Hurdler

Some people think that fences should be seen and not hurdled! Others float gracefully over them. Here, however, we have a hurdler who is making a bit of a mess of it. Still, he gets full marks for effort.

These two rounded shapes start you off with head and body.

This inner oval marks out the division between vest and shorts.

Add this blob for one leg, which is bent behind the runner and so appears short. Draw a longer, sausage-like shape for the leading leg.

This bulge gives you part of the right arm, mostly hidden behind the runner. Draw the other arm swinging forward, and add big, shapeless feet to the legs.

Now the whole figure is sketched in, you can add the hurdles – which he is only just clearing. The back hurdle is drawn on a slant, as it is toppling over. Too close for comfort!

The face fits within your original oval: you only need add a small bulge for the nose. Add a curve to suggest the puffed-out cheeks.

Making the hair stream jaggedly behind him is an effective way of giving the impression of speed.

His hand is clenched into a fist with the effort of hurdling.

A couple of creases add shape to his running vest.

Who was the fastest runner in history?

Adam, of course. He was the first in the human race.

Cricketer

Cricket can be a dangerous game, as this batsman has just discovered. He has hit the ball fair and square, but the ball doesn't seem to observe the rules of the game! Perhaps the bowler used a cannonball by mistake!

Two slanting ovals form the batsman's head and body.

Add two elongated ovals to outline his legs. The back leg is slightly shorter, because of the angle at which we see it.

Shape this arm carefully, setting the elbow halfway down the body. Padded gloves make the hands big and rather shapeless.

Finish off his legs which are protected by pads, and add large feet.

Behind the two lumpy gloves, these two shapes form his other arm and sleeve.

Draw the bat, with a hole in the middle.

Draw round, staring eyes and a mouth twisted in dismay.

Shape the large pads that are made of individual sections.

The wind of the ball's flight has flicked up his collar.

Even the wicket is falling apart with surprise!

Canoeist

Water provides opportunities for all sorts of sports, from water-skiing to fishing. Paddling your own canoe is one way to enjoy yourself on the water. Being pursued by sharks isn't! Put the two together and you have an unusual experience! Jaws with oars!

Start with the head and body and then, a little way off, outline the blades of the paddle.

Next, draw in the hollow canopy of the canoe.

Start the right arm at the center of the body, with the left one just above it.

Make the bunches of hair slightly uneven.

Curve the lower part of the body where it fits into the canoe seat.

American Footballer

American football is a rough, tough contact sport. The players look hugely powerful in their protective clothing. But sometimes people who are tough on the outside can be quite timid really, when faced with a spider — or a mouse!

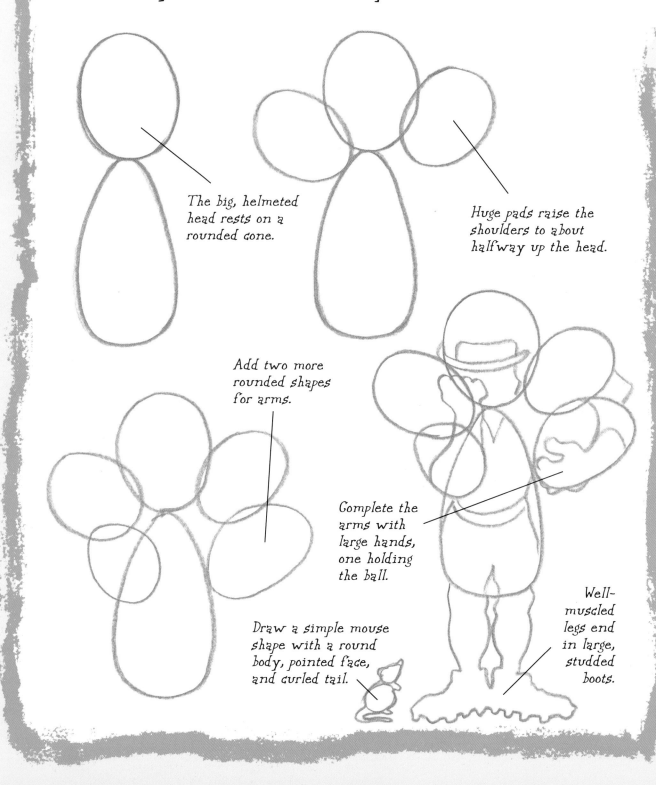

The big, helmeted head rests on a rounded cone.

Huge pads raise the shoulders to about halfway up the head.

Add two more rounded shapes for arms.

Complete the arms with large hands, one holding the ball.

Draw a simple mouse shape with a round body, pointed face, and curled tail.

Well-muscled legs end in large, studded boots.

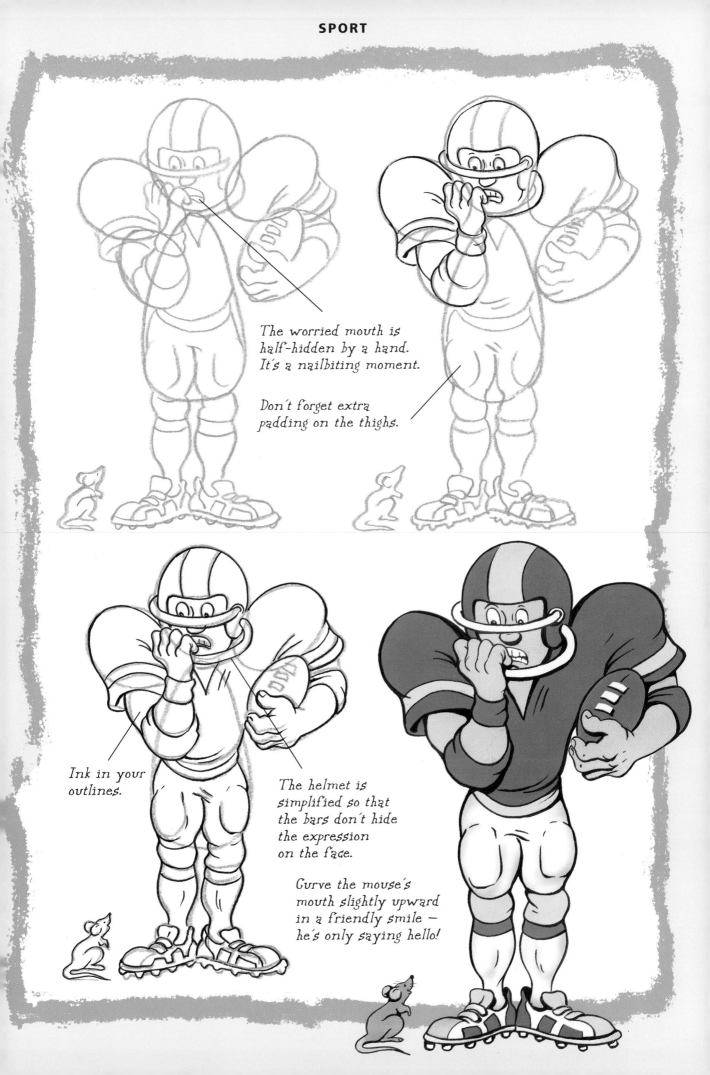

The worried mouth is
half-hidden by a hand.
It's a nailbiting moment.

Don't forget extra
padding on the thighs.

Ink in your
outlines.

The helmet is
simplified so that
the bars don't hide
the expression
on the face.

Curve the mouse's
mouth slightly upward
in a friendly smile —
he's only saying hello!

Rugby Player

You don't have to draw a whole rugby team to capture the speed and excitement of the game. One player in action is enough to represent all of them. Of course, it helps to exaggerate his brute strength.

This circle isn't his head, but his powerful shoulder, thrusting for the line.

These two odd shapes form his body, twisted as he changes direction.

This is the head, with bulging cheeks puffed out to the sides.

Add the bent arm, cradling the ball in a giant grasp.

His large feet are positioned well to the side. Leave a good space for the legs.

Link the feet to the body with strong, muscular legs.

The clenched jaw stretches his face into a grimace of exertion.

The wide sleeve balloons out round his arm.

Draw in his socks and rugby boots.

His hair stands up in a crown of spikes.

The H-shaped goalposts are just visible behind his shoulder.

The twist of his body, pushing ahead of his legs, adds to the impression of speed.

Surfer

Sun, sea, and sand will do for most of us. But for athletic types like this guy, it has to be sun, sea, and surf! It takes a good sense of balance, but you're never bored with a board while there are waves to ride.

The head perches on a body that is leaning back to maintain his balance.

The two oval shapes for his thighs come to a point at the knees. They are both bigger than the head, because they are nearer to us in this view.

A little way below the thigh, add the outline of a foot, placed sideways.

This blunt-cornered triangle will help you to position his bent arm, raised toward his head.

When you draw this outstretched arm, place it so that the shoulder pushes upward from the body, to emphasize the muscles.

Only one end of the surfboard emerges from the rolling waves. Finish shaping the legs, and add a wave breaking over the back of the board.

Windswept hair streams behind him. Now you can add detail to the bent arm, curling the fingers round into a clenched fist.

Draw in the face, making the huge, happy grin the main feature. Don't forget the dimple in his chin. What a dude!

Draw splashing waves all around the surfboard, and add a few flying, tear-shaped drops of water.

Give him a muscular chest to match the curving muscles of his arms and legs. (But he can still have knobbly knees.)

Why do surfers never have hidden depths?

Because they're all surf aces!

Complete his feet with broad toes, bracing themselves on the curved board.

Pegasus

In Greek myth, the winged horse Pegasus roams the skies freely. Only the gods and (with their permission) heroes dare ride him. But the cartoon world can be a gentler place, where he becomes a happy colt scampering among the clouds.

Your starting point is these three circles — space them carefully.

This kite-like shape forms a wing. Take care with the angles!

Shape the wing by curving the outer edges inward.

Link the circles with a broad neck, and add two pricked ears.

Add these small circles to form the leg joints, and attach a flowing tail.

Now draw the muzzle, with a large nostril and the mouth open in a happy smile. Add a thick mane.

Draw in the legs and hoofs.

Curve the join between muzzle and head, and draw in details of eyes, ears, and wings. Short lines beside the wings and tails give the impression of movement.

Finish drawing the head and shaggy mane.

Fluffy clouds adorn the skies which are Pegasus's playground.

Shape the base of the wing where it sprouts from the shoulder, and ink in your outlines.

Cartoon animals often have large heads to make a stronger impact. The downward glance in the eye helps give an impression that Pegasus is flying high.

Bad Fairy

Long ago, bad fairies were really scary. People blamed them for any illness or bad luck, and dreaded offending them. Today the Bad Fairy belongs only in fairy stories and pantomimes, where her wicked ways are always easily defeated.

The head is a fat oval — not a circle! Draw a curved line across it, about a third of the way down.

Add a small, solid body and two bent 'stick' arms.

A big 'shark's fin' shape forms the hat.

Draw a big topless triangle to make guidelines for the wings, and add 'stick' legs.

Now start adding details. Shape the arms, legs, and hat, draw in the wings, and add slanted eyes and a snub nose.

The slant of the evil grin matches that of the eyes.

The huge hat adds to the comic, cartoon effect. Its pointy shape also suggests the hat of another fairy-tale baddie, the Wicked Witch.

Draw the hair with jagged, spiky lines as you ink in your cartoon.

Keep the feet small, with simple boots.

Fairy wings are transparent, like those of an insect.

Good Fairy

With a wave of her magic wand, the Good Fairy makes everything come right. Let's draw her and her wand in action. Cartoon actions are always exaggerated, so she bends and braces herself as if the wand were a big, heavy club.

Start off with three carefully placed circles.

Straight lines mark out the shape of the wings.

Draw curved lines as a guide for positioning the legs.

Set her crown at an angle.

The two pairs of wings are shaped like those of a dragonfly.

A slanted line forms both arm and wand.

Draw in the legs, spread wide to balance her body.

Add a star at the tip of the wand.

Sketch in some fairy boots.

Her head is tilted, so draw eyes and mouth on a slant.

Curve her dress smoothly around her legs.

Wide, level eyes, a small nose, and a smiling mouth make up a very different face from the Bad Fairy's.

A trail of little sparkling stars shows the wand's movement.

Both hands meet at the end of the wand.

Bad Fairies have to wear black or dark shades, but white or light colors form the Good Fairy's 'uniform.'

Genie of the Lamp

When Aladdin rubbed his magic lamp, out came the Genie to grant his wishes. And here he comes again, in a puff of smoke.

Draw the head first, with a large 'slice' marked out to separate face from turban.

The circles and curved line establish the arms and hands.

The puff of smoke is nearly as big as his head.

The lamp goes here.

Now link up your three sections and your Genie starts to appear.

Draw the lamp like a squashed teapot with a long spout.

Give him a happy grin showing big front teeth.

Slanting lines show the folds of his flowing cloak.

Curving the fingers helps to suggest movement.

Use small curves to fluff out the cloud of smoke.

As if by magic your Genie has appeared. 'What is your command, O master?'

Wicked Witch

Cartoon witches are instantly recognizable by their pointy hats. They also have long chins and long noses, warts and claw-like hands. If they aren't flying on a broomstick, they are usually cooking up some horrible spell in a caldron.

This is less complicated than it looks! A few more lines give you the hat brim, a fall of greasy hair, and two raised hands.

These three odd shapes don't look much like a witch yet!

Draw the pointy top of the hat.

Add a big nose, draw in the sleeves and fingers, and suddenly the witch starts to appear.

Turn the lower oval into the rim of a caldron, and add curved sides and a handle. Above it, the Witch's hands hover like bird's claws.

Why did the witch spin round and round?

Because she was having a dizzy spell!

Narrow, curving eyes perch either side of the nose. Sketch in an evil grin, and don't forget the warts!

As you start to ink in your cartoon, make your Wicked Witch look as evil as possible.

Have fun inking in the details, making fingers knobblier and hair stragglier.

A few lumps in the caldron hint at something even worse than school meals!

By drawing the pupils at the outer edges of the eyes, you can make it seem as if the witch is looking — and grinning — directly at you.

What does a witch wear in the kitchen?

Coven gloves!

Dragon

Dragons are among the oldest inhabitants of the fantasy world. You can have some fun with their fire-breathing habits — this dragon is having problems trying to read a newspaper. He should know about the dangers of smoking!

Start with a circle, and a larger egg shape. Leave a generous space between the two.

Now add a 'tear drop,' overlapping both your first shapes. This is the dragon's long snout.

Draw in the edges of the newspaper.

Two slanting ovals form the hind legs.

Give your dragon three horns, and add eyes and nostrils.

Add a strong, stout tail, coiled behind the leg and ending in a pointed shape.

Goblin

Goblins aren't nice. Small, hideous, and spiteful, they belong to the dark side of the fairy world. In the days before street lights, they lurked on every dark corner.

Start with this shape — an egg with a pointed end — and add a 'skirt.'

Add these four shapes below, for hands and feet.

Start to draw in the goblin's club.

A big lump of a nose and pointed ears help to form a goblin face. Join on the arms, just below the ears.

Shape the shoes, and add little bandy legs.

He carries a simple 'Stone Age' club, ready for action.

The fleshy nose is the key to this face. The upper lip follows its curve, and the eyes tuck in against the top slopes.

Sketch in a small tufty beard.

All the detail is concentrated in the face. The staring eyes look mean. A few sharp teeth hang over the lower lip, ready to give someone a nasty nip.

Keep clothing simple — goblins aren't snazzy dressers!

The angle of the feet and the shortened body make it seem as if we are looking down on the goblin from above. Watch out for your ankles!

Maw

You can make a splendid monster by taking just one feature — from a nose to a foot — and concentrating simply on that. This monster is all mouth, to go with its monster appetite.

Start with a rough egg shape, tilted to one side.

Ovals for feet are linked to the body by a curved line.

The huge mouth takes up most of the egg shape. Sketch an oval on top, and add eyes and nose.

A central circle forms a dangly tonsil. Sketch two rings round it, like a target, to help you build up the inside of the mouth.

Mark out the teeth with large ovals.

Make-believe creatures don't need to have matching eyes. Goggle eyes look great!

These two ovals form the tongue, with a grooved center.

Build up layers within the mouth to give the impression of cavernous depths.

Maw food, please!

The feet are like spanners lying flat on the ground.

Scrabber

Some monsters are inspired by real-life beasties. Think of a crab. It's an odd shape to start with — a sort of walking plate with jaws. Multiply the eyes, add some tongues, take away a couple of legs, and what have you got? Well, we've called our monster a Scrabber.

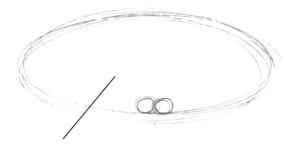

Start with a long oval for the body. Put two small eyes at the front.

Add half a dozen legs, with big oval feet.

Decorate the 'knees' with oval blobs.

Add a generous helping of loony eyes and tongues.

Sketch in some toes.

Give him a wide, friendly smile — you wouldn't want him to be unfriendly!

The back feet are partly hidden behind the middle legs.

Try out some toenails — or maybe claws.

Decorate the back. These could become scales, or just be a spotted pattern.

When you ink in your outlines, use thicker blotches to adorn the legs and shape the feet.

A few short spikes on the back and legs complete the Scrabber.

Flump

As a general rule, thin spiky monsters look dangerous, and fat rounded ones look cuddly. Try out the thoroughly rounded Flump and see what you think. Cuddly or not, I'm not sure I want to find a Flump lurking under my bed!

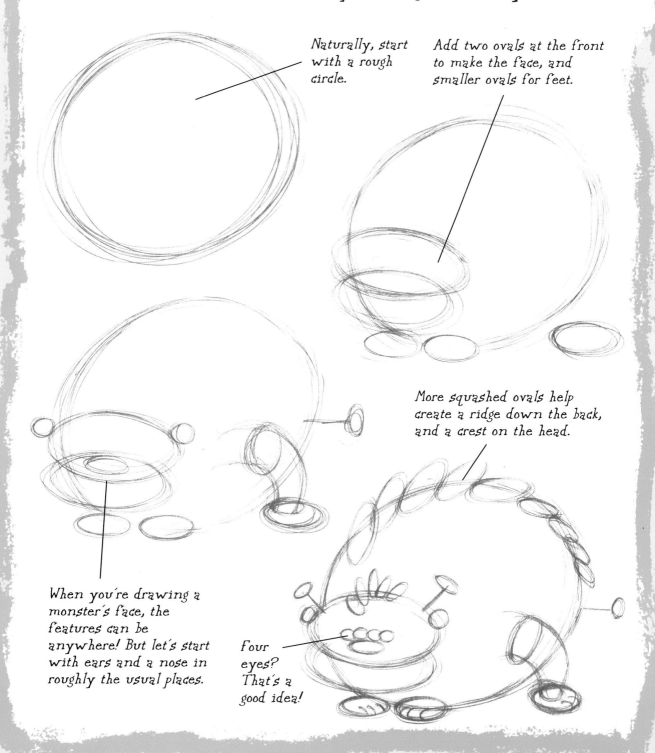

Naturally, start with a rough circle.

Add two ovals at the front to make the face, and smaller ovals for feet.

More squashed ovals help create a ridge down the back, and a crest on the head.

When you're drawing a monster's face, the features can be anywhere! But let's start with ears and a nose in roughly the usual places.

Four eyes? That's a good idea!

Finish drawing the head.
A huge, frilly tongue
hanging out of the mouth
makes a change from
monstrous teeth.

Decorate the
Flump with a
scattering of
spots on the back
and legs.

A monster can have any
number of eyes you
want — and they don't
have to match!

Some tails hang down, some
stick up. The one thing they
never do in real life is stick
straight out behind. So what
does a monster's tail do?
You've got it!

What's a monster's
favorite meal?

Human beans!

(Of course, if they
see him coming,
they'll probably be
runner beans!)

Slugg

The common-or-garden slug is a mini-monster in the eyes of the squeamish — and of any gardener. You can build on this real-life creepy-crawly to create the monstrous Slugg, complete with horns, wings, and a toothy grin.

Build up the body in three parts, overlapping the base of the shape that makes the head.

The head is an egg shape with two eyes on top.

The small wing sprouts on a stalk from the middle of the back.

Start putting in details. Fringe the smile with teeth, add small horns below the eyes, and sketch in wing feathers. This is a weird one!

Shape the join between head and chest into the smooth curves of a long neck.

Ugliness is only skin-deep. Of course, some monsters have awfully thick skins!

Decorate the chest with a pattern of spots, and do the same down the back. If you make the spots different shapes — circles and ovals — they will look more interesting.

Draw in a single eyebrow floating above the head.

Have you ever seen odder-looking wings?

The tail curls upward, like a happy dog's.

Make the underneath of the Slugg wavy, rather than straight, to show how it ripples along the ground.

A shadow at the base of the neck helps to make the head look heavy and solid.

The Slugg isn't altogether a new invention. In ancient times it would have been classified as a Worm, or Wyrm, a kind of slimy legless dragon.

Ogre

The ogre is the nastiest kind of giant. He eats people but, luckily for the heroes who have to deal with ogres, he isn't usually very bright.

This oval builds up the head with a heavy jaw — all the better to eat you with!

Build up your drawing round this circle.

Drape the arms round the body in a horseshoe shape.

This blob marks the site of the eyes.

A row of ugly teeth runs across the center of the face.

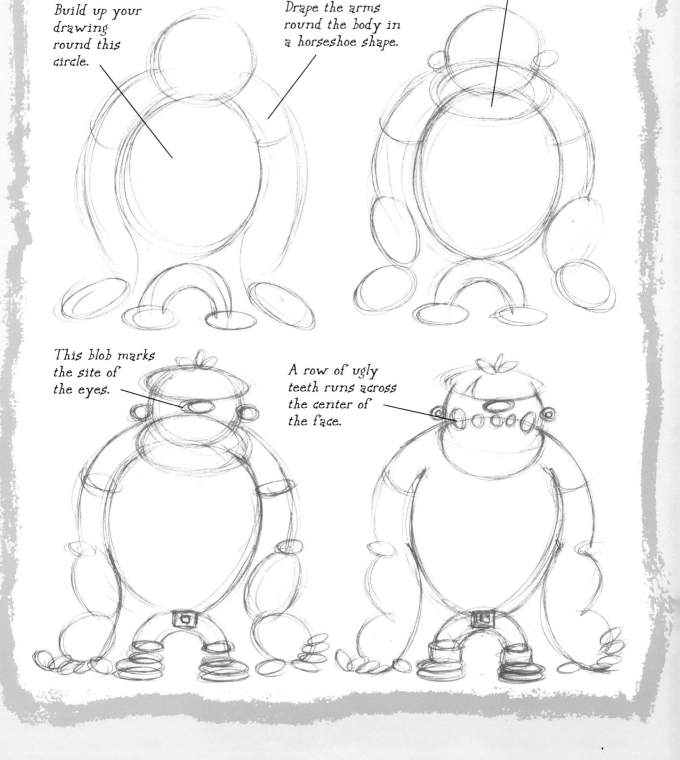

Shape the hair, with a fringe.

Huge arms bulge with muscles and the knuckles trail on the ground.

Comical little legs end in short, round feet.

Cartoons exaggerate important features. So the dangerous bits — head, arms, and stomach (think about it!) — are huge, while the legs are the smallest part of the drawing.

This guy's mouth is watering. Get ready to run for it.

Keep clothes simple: trousers, T-shirt, and a single decorative touch, the belt buckle.

The hero said to the ogre, 'Your stomach is enormous. You should diet!'

And the ogre replied, 'Okay. What color?'

Blobb

Monsters don't have to be shapely — they can be as blobby as you like. Here's what happens when you start with a simple idea and add a few teeth and tentacles. The Blobb isn't a very scary monster — unless you imagine it the size of a house!

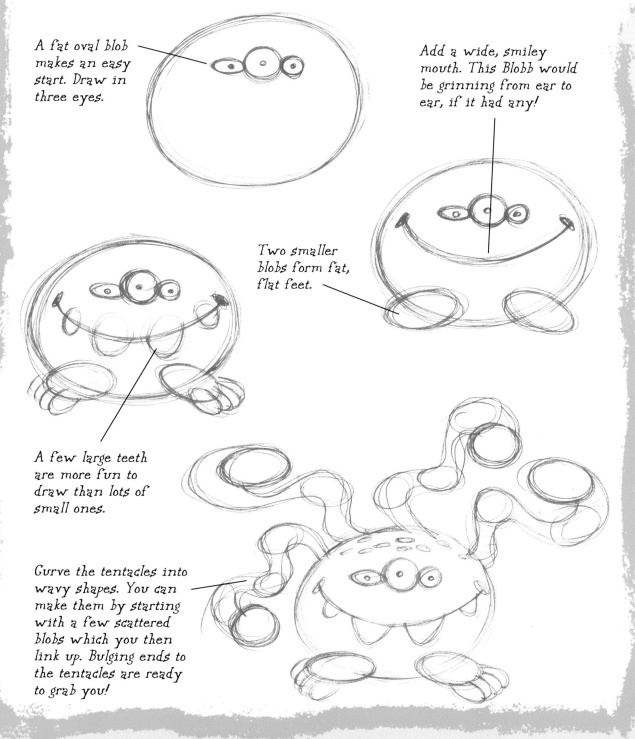

A fat oval blob makes an easy start. Draw in three eyes.

Add a wide, smiley mouth. This Blobb would be grinning from ear to ear, if it had any!

Two smaller blobs form fat, flat feet.

A few large teeth are more fun to draw than lots of small ones.

Curve the tentacles into wavy shapes. You can make them by starting with a few scattered blobs which you then link up. Bulging ends to the tentacles are ready to grab you!

Dapple the forehead with a few spots or splatters.

This monster's got no nose.

How does he smell?

Awful!

Small shadows behind the eyes give them depth.

Curving shadows within the tentacles help to make them look solid.

Is he waving hello, or should you be waving goodbye?

Frankenstein's Monster

Frankenstein was so keen on Do-It-Yourself that he built his own monster out of bits and pieces. But it didn't work very well! And, as you can see, he wasn't too good at needlework. His stitches had to be reinforced with bolts.

Sketch out the rough shape with curved lines.

Curved lines establish a heavy jaw and mouth

Two ovals help to form built-up boots.

Draw in the collar and buttons, and the whole jacket begins to take shape.

Make the hands enormous. The monster is made out of bits of different people, and they don't fit together very well. It makes you wonder why Frankenstein didn't wait to collect a matching set of pieces.

Draw in a line of stitches round the neck, and start drawing the metal nuts and bolts on either side.

Small close-set eyes stare straight ahead from under a single eyebrow.

Try drawing the shading as a bold zig-zag pattern.

The legs are braced apart, showing that it is an effort for this monster to walk.

Where does Frankenstein keep his money?

In an organ bank!

Fishface

Monsters can be as monstrous as you like. You can take bits and pieces from all sorts of ideas and mix them together. What happens if you combine a big round head, human arms, and a fish's tail? Let's put them together and see!

These simple shapes make a start.

A couple of ovals help form the tail.

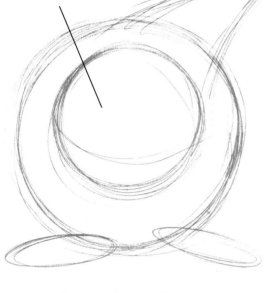 

A smaller oval below the head establishes a gap between the arms, almost closed at the base by the outstretched thumbs.

Draw in the jacket — although perhaps he should be wearing a 'tail' coat?

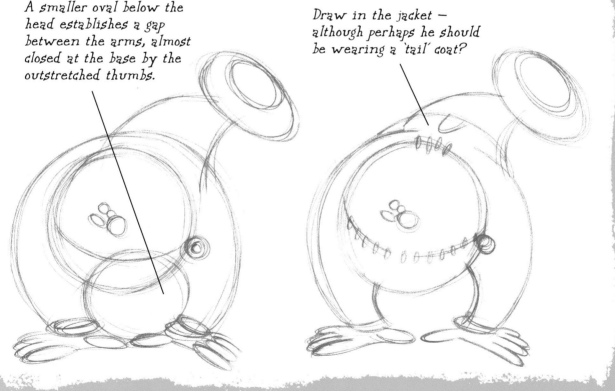

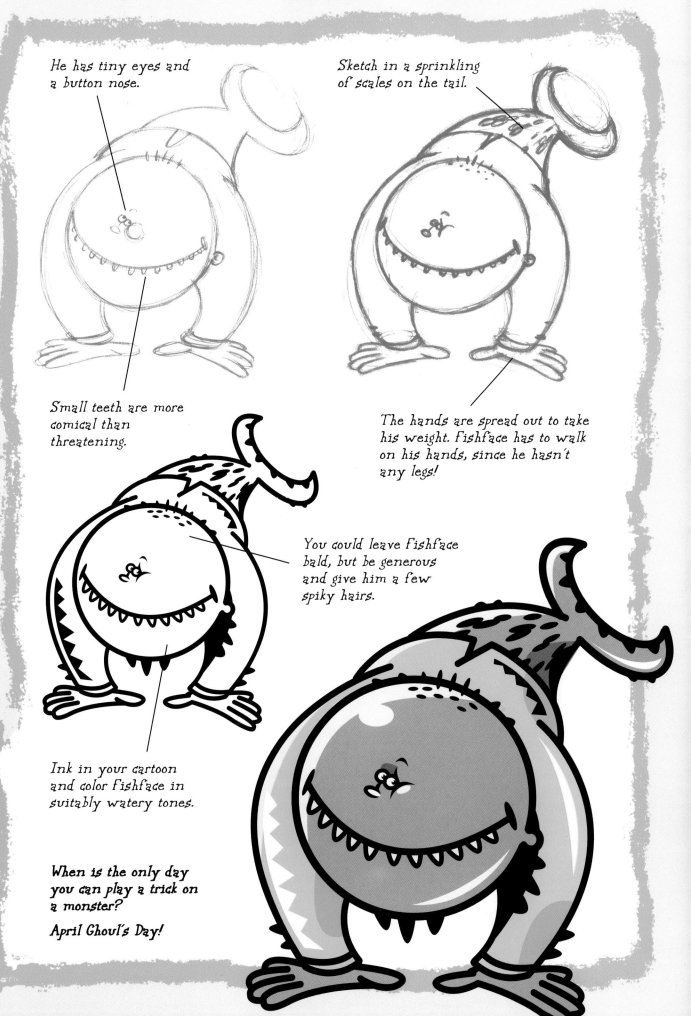

He has tiny eyes and a button nose.

Sketch in a sprinkling of scales on the tail.

Small teeth are more comical than threatening.

The hands are spread out to take his weight. Fishface has to walk on his hands, since he hasn't any legs!

You could leave Fishface bald, but be generous and give him a few spiky hairs.

Ink in your cartoon and color Fishface in suitably watery tones.

When is the only day you can play a trick on a monster?

April Ghoul's Day!

Sun With Hat On

To scientists, the Sun is a ball of burning gas. Artists often prefer to depict it as a smiling golden face surrounded by bright rays. All we need to do is dress this up a little, with hat and gloves, to create a jolly cartoon Sun.

Start with the round face, crowned by a rough oval for the hat brim.

Hat and brim together are the same height as the whole face.

Draw in the hatband.

In cartoons, hands are often drawn with only three fingers (and a thumb).

Little flames fringe the edges to form the Sun's rays — and, at the same time, make a beard to finish off the face.

Ignore the lower curve of the
hat when drawing the face —
this was just a guideline to help
you position the hat brim.

Ink in the outlines of the hat
with flowing curves. The hand
on the brim is raising the hat
in greeting.

Below the mouth, draw
a jolly double chin.

For a welcoming smile, the
mouth curves up in the center
as well as at the corners.

In the words of the old song:
'The sun has got his hat on —
hip, hip, hip, hooray!'

I got up at dawn this
morning to see the sunrise.

Well, you couldn't have
picked a better time!

Meteorite

A meteorite is a piece of rock that comes blasting out of space. If it hits Earth, it lands with a real bang. Most meteorites miss Earth, but the one in this drawing has every intention of hitting something — or somebody!

Draw a rough circle, not a perfect one — rocks aren't naturally round!

Small fragments break off as the meteorite hurtles through space.

Shape the eyes like orange segments.

This teardrop shape forms half of the fierce, scowling mouth.

Draw a squashed nose between the lower corners of the eyes. A similar curve completes the mouth.

These curves suggest heavy eyebrows.

As you ink in the features, start adding little dots and streaks to create the rough texture of rock.

Use wavy lines and curves, not sharp zig-zags, to make the outline rough and lumpy.

Teeth can be suggested quite easily with straight lines.

'Where should I park the rocket, man?'

'Wherever you see a space, man.'

Saturn

Nine planets (including Earth) orbit the Sun. Everybody recognizes Saturn, because of its famous rings. Actually, three other planets have rings too — but nobody remembers that, because Saturn's are so much more spectacular.

Draw this long shape across the center of the circle for the rings.

Start by drawing a simple circle.

A smaller shape within the long one will create a hollow center to the rings.

Just below the rings, place three small ovals — the eyes and nose of Saturn's face.

Now you can draw the whole face. Make the features big enough to occupy all the space below the rings.

Don't ink in the upper part of the rings, which will be hidden behind Saturn's face. You can rub out these pencil guidelines later.

Smile lines around the eyes help to give the face a kindly expression. A little chin juts out at the bottom.

Saturn's many shimmering rings, made up of ice and dust, are simplified here into a single ring. A star-filled night sky behind completes the heavenly scene.

Small Robot

Robots can boldly go where humans can't. This makes them very useful in space, so movies about space travel often feature walking, talking robots. Small robots tend to look rather appealing to us, as if we think of them as cute pets.

The head is almost as big as the squat, chunky body.

Draw the jointed arms using two ovals for each.

Three little curves on top of the head mimic hair.

The feet form a wide base, so the robot will not topple over easily.

These two shape form pincer 'hands.'

Small rectangles for eyes, and straight lines for eyebrows and mouth, make this a mechanical face, not a human one.

Use straight lines to draw in the body panels.

Draw big bolts at the joints of the arms where sections overlap.

Why are robots never afraid?

Because they have nerves of steel.

Crescent Moon

The Moon is much more than just a lump of rock in the sky. Its silvery light and changing shape make it seem magical. Some people see a face in its surface: the Man in the Moon. On the other hand, others see a rabbit there instead!

Draw your Moon, with the bulge of a face and nose just above the center.

Draw this circle (the spaceman's head) about its own diameter away from the Moon.

How can you tell that the Moon is pleased to see you?

The Moon beams.

Two more ovals complete his body. Add arms with big gloved hands, and the far leg. A circle within the head shape gives you the face within the clear helmet.

These four small ovals form the lower part of the spaceman's body, and his large boots.

Just above the Moon's nose, draw a large oval eye, nearly as big as the nose.

Sketch in the spaceman's face, giving him a big, friendly grin.

Finish drawing the Moon's face. When you draw in the eye, place the pupil quite low down so that the Moon is looking downward, directly at his visitor.

Ink in your outlines. Make sure you have the spaceman's face looking up at the Moon. All those ovals you used to draw his body help to create the shape of his bouncy spacesuit now.

When you color in your drawing, use shading to give a rounded look to the sections of the spacesuit. And add some twinkling stars in the background.

Merry Martian

People can't agree on whether aliens exist somewhere out in space, let alone what they look like if they do! This means you can have fun designing your own aliens. You can make them any shape you like — and nobody can prove you're wrong!

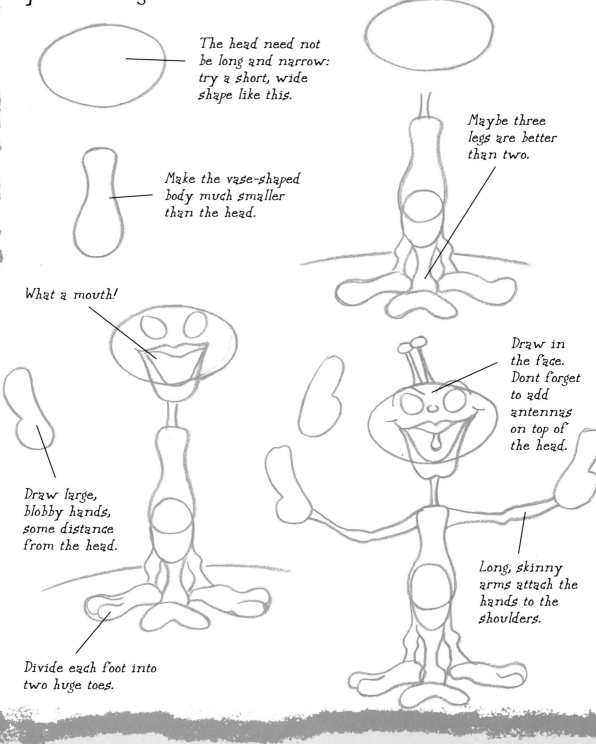

The head need not be long and narrow: try a short, wide shape like this.

Maybe three legs are better than two.

Make the vase-shaped body much smaller than the head.

What a mouth!

Draw in the face. Dont forget to add antennas on top of the head.

Draw large, blobby hands, some distance from the head.

Long, skinny arms attach the hands to the shoulders.

Divide each foot into two huge toes.

Rocket Rider

A cartoonist can draw the impossible. You may be inspired to reverse the way things usually are. An astronaut travels inside a large rocket. Turn this round and imagine him riding on the outside of a small rocket. Not very comfortable — but fun to draw!

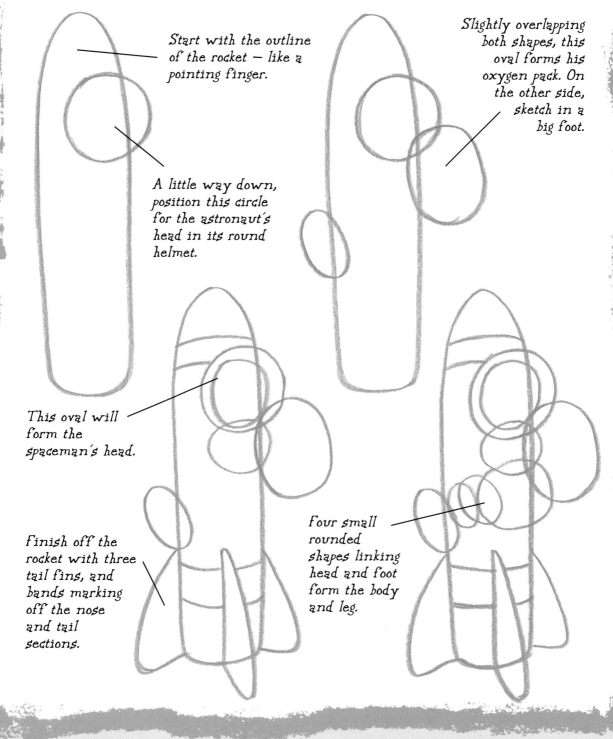

Start with the outline of the rocket — like a pointing finger.

A little way down, position this circle for the astronaut's head in its round helmet.

Slightly overlapping both shapes, this oval forms his oxygen pack. On the other side, sketch in a big foot.

This oval will form the spaceman's head.

Finish off the rocket with three tail fins, and bands marking off the nose and tail sections.

Four small rounded shapes linking head and foot form the body and leg.

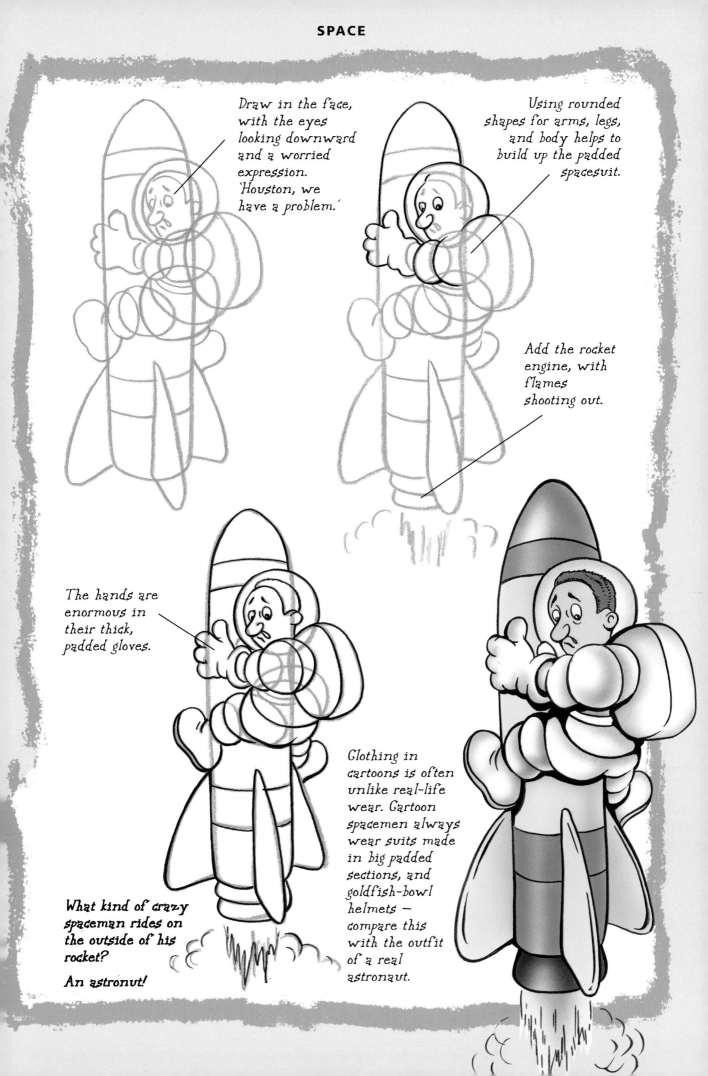

Draw in the face, with the eyes looking downward and a worried expression. 'Houston, we have a problem.'

Using rounded shapes for arms, legs, and body helps to build up the padded spacesuit.

Add the rocket engine, with flames shooting out.

The hands are enormous in their thick, padded gloves.

Glothing in cartoons is often unlike real-life wear. Cartoon spacemen always wear suits made in big padded sections, and goldfish-bowl helmets — compare this with the outfit of a real astronaut.

What kind of crazy spaceman rides on the outside of his rocket?

An astronut!

Moon-Walking

When the first astronaut took 'one giant step for mankind' on the surface of the Moon, this isn't quite what he meant! Swapping round the sizes of Moon and astronaut produces a great comic effect. Giving the Moon a face helps, too!

Start with a good big circle for the Moon.

Two small overlapping circles form the astronaut's head and body.

Give the Moon eyes and a smiling mouth.

Finish off the astronaut. Placing his arms outstretched shows that he is having to work at keeping his balance on the Moon.

Keep the face simple.

The astronaut has planted a flag.

Add some detail to the Moon's facial features. Those are craters, not freckles!

The Moon's eyes are turned upward to see who is dancing on his head. A wide smile welcomes the Earthling.

Small crescents depict craters on the Moon's surface.

Make the Moon's outline a little uneven, to represent the rough surface.

Bully Boy

A caricature can express your opinion of someone. The bully thinks his physical strength makes him important. But by drawing him with a huge head on a small body, you can make his mean expression more significant than his muscles.

Start with a big egg shape for the head.

The emphasis in this drawing is on the head. The body is drawn much smaller, so you need only add a small square below the head for the torso.

The ears are normally shaped, but stick out more than usual.

This curve marks out eyebrows drawn down in a scowl.

Draw one and a half legs — the short leg is bent in the action of running.

Make the arms small and simple. Sketch the hands as blocks, because they are clenched into fists.

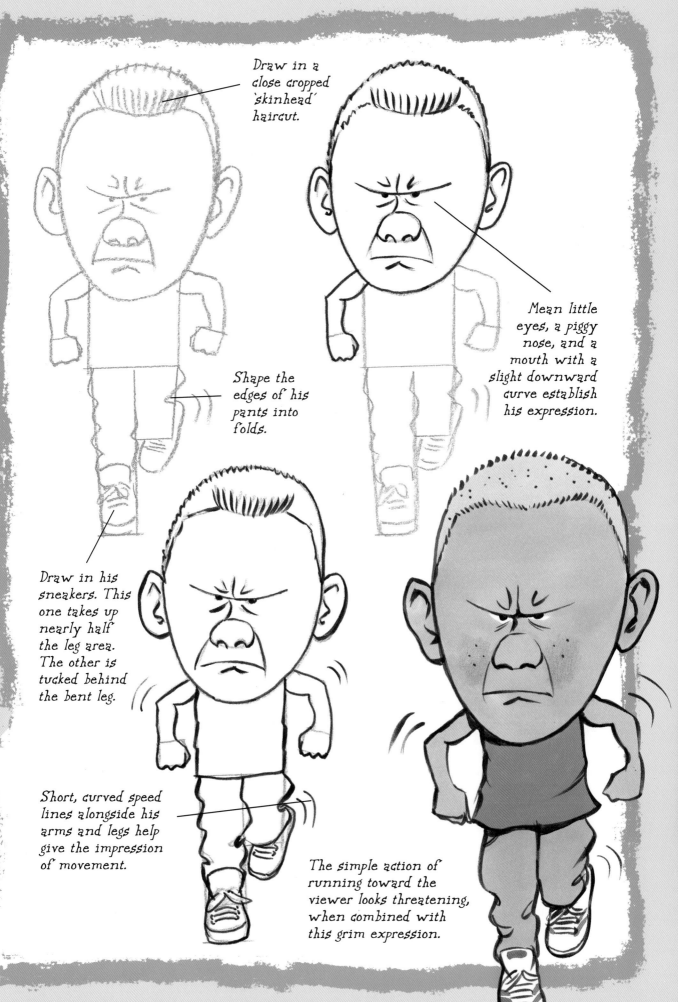

Draw in a close cropped 'skinhead' haircut.

Mean little eyes, a piggy nose, and a mouth with a slight downward curve establish his expression.

Shape the edges of his pants into folds.

Draw in his sneakers. This one takes up nearly half the leg area. The other is tucked behind the bent leg.

Short, curved speed lines alongside his arms and legs help give the impression of movement.

The simple action of running toward the viewer looks threatening, when combined with this grim expression.

Soccer Star

Goal! Soccer players don't hide their feelings when they score a goal. Here we capture that moment of celebration. Note how an impression of excitement is given by drawing the figure tilted over at an angle, rather than upright.

A rectangle forms the top of the head.

On either side of your central slanting line, draw these long narrow triangles, like wings. They form the outstretched arms.

Make this triangle the same length as the oblong at the top. It forms the area for the chin and open mouth.

Draw a broad nose on the center line of the face. Divide the lower face with slanting lines, and add large ears to either side.

Below the chest, add a small pair of shorts. Now turn the trailing section of your long slanting line into a leg.

A huge grin dominates the face.

The arms occupy only the lower part of the guideline triangles.

This leg appears only half the length of the other, because it is bent backward, making it look shorter. Speed marks beside the leg help to give an impression of movement.

The goal looks small because it is in the distance, behind the running player. Don't forget to put in the ball — the reason for the player's delight!

Ink in your drawing and color your cartoon soccer star in your favorite team's strip.

Captain: Why didn't you save the ball?

Goalkeeper: What do you think the nets are for?

Disc Jockey

Another approach to caricature is to link the person's appearance to that of the tools of his trade. Here, the disc jockey is drawn with a big, round head and straight, narrow body. His shape mimics that of the microphone he uses!

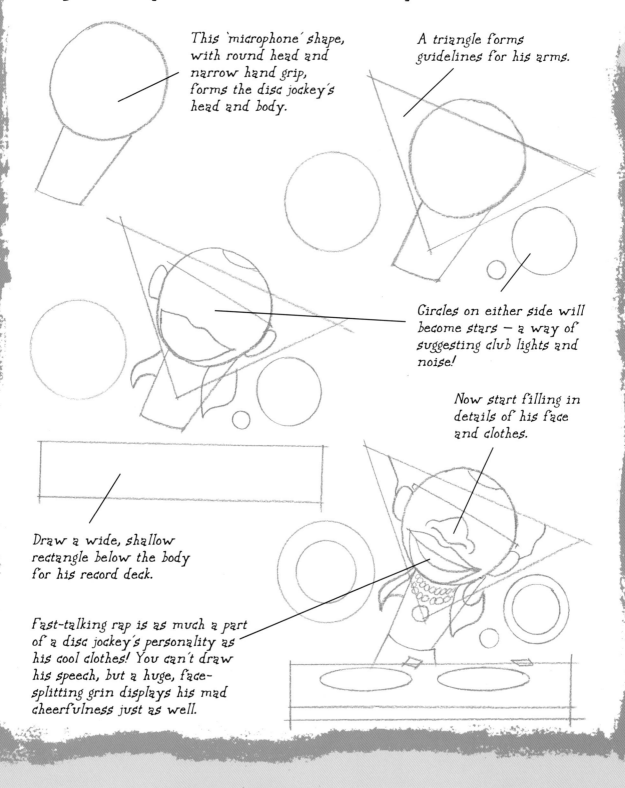

This 'microphone' shape, with round head and narrow hand grip, forms the disc jockey's head and body.

A triangle forms guidelines for his arms.

Circles on either side will become stars — a way of suggesting club lights and noise!

Now start filling in details of his face and clothes.

Draw a wide, shallow rectangle below the body for his record deck.

Fast-talking rap is as much a part of a disc jockey's personality as his cool clothes! You can't draw his speech, but a huge, face-splitting grin displays his mad cheerfulness just as well.

Under a pair of simple eyebrows, draw the outline of large, wraparound dark glasses. These will hide his eyes and reflect the spotlights.

Keep the deck simple. Many DJs have complex, flashy equipment, but you don't want to distract attention from the main man.

Use your triangle to position the short, thin arms, and the hands with their pointing fingers.

Shape the edges of your circles into jagged edges to form stars. Giving one straight edges and the other curved makes a zappy effect.

My father asked if the disc jockey would play requests?

I told him, 'Yes, of course.' He said, 'Then ask him to play chess!'

Butler

The joke about butlers in cartoons (and often in films and books) is that they are usually much grander than their employers. Smart clothes, highly polished shoes, and a snooty expression are essential!

The head is long and tilted back to create a 'nose in the air' expression.

The body and front leg are tilted too, but at a slightly less steep angle than the head. Slanted lines across the trouser bottoms mark the tops of his shoes.

The cover of his serving dish is easily drawn as a half-circle.

Draw a large 'shark-fin' shape for his nose that is held haughtily in the air.

The arm fits neatly within the shape of the body.

Sketch in his jacket, with its long tails.

Finish his trouser bottoms with curving lines, leaving a space above the shoes for his white spats.

Start to fill in the details of his face and add a serving handle to the silver dish.

Start to ink in your cartoon. Just a few well-chosen details can create a very convincing character.

Use curved lines to give a more natural shape to his trousers, and draw in his shoes and white spats.

Ink in your outlines keeping your cartoon smart and stylish — just like the butler himself!

Small 'action' lines will make your cartoon butler look as if he is walking.

'Jeeves, there's a fly in my soup.'

'What's it doing there, sir?'

'Breaststroke, I think!'

Horsewoman

You can caricature people by making them look like their interests. Some really do! In cartoons at least, 'horsey' people always resemble their beloved horses. A laughing mouth full of huge teeth is a must, and so of course is a pony-tail!

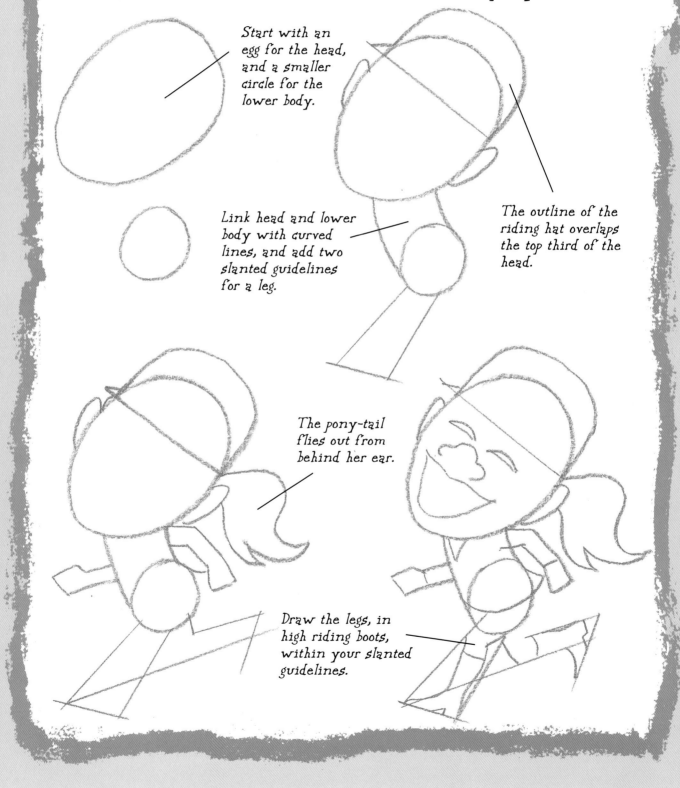

Start with an egg for the head, and a smaller circle for the lower body.

Link head and lower body with curved lines, and add two slanted guidelines for a leg.

The outline of the riding hat overlaps the top third of the head.

The pony-tail flies out from behind her ear.

Draw the legs, in high riding boots, within your slanted guidelines.

Large features fill most of the face. Those teeth look big enough to tackle a nosebag!

People who spend much of their time outdoors often have eyes narrowed from squinting into the sun.

The back of the jacket trails out toward the hand.

A riding crop is the easiest bit of horsey kit to draw!

Riding kit is simple: a smart jacket, jodhpurs, and high boots.

The horsewoman is as active as her pony, moving along at a brisk trot.

Firefighter

Tools can be very tricky things. Even an ordinary hose can tie the user in knots — imagine what a firefighter's equipment can get up to! And, of course, in the world of cartoons things can go much further than in real life!

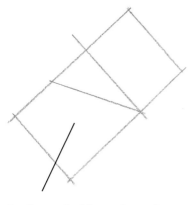

The kicking legs can be drawn as a simple 'V' shape.

A slanted oblong doesn't look much like a firefighter's head and body; but just wait. Two lines across it mark out his helmet and arm.

Curve the back and base of the body. Cut off the corners of the helmet to give it a more rounded shape, and curve the brim.

Waving arms and outstretched hands show how he is trying to regain his balance.

The waterspout spills round him like the petals of a giant flower. Add the jet and the nozzle of the hose at the base.

Finish off his legs with boots. Below the waterspout, draw in a looping line for the hose.

Draw the shocked face and characteristic helmet with its high crest.

Creases in his jacket under his elbow show how his body is bent in two by the force of the water.

Draw in the hose, with a few 'spin' marks to show movement.

His arms and legs flail wildly in different directions.

A few drops of flying water help to make the whole cartoon look even wetter!

Water shoots out of a fire hose at high pressure — maybe it could support a man!

Sailor

Some sailors can hit the rocks even on dry land. After an enjoyable voyage, this one is tying up his boat and what happens? A cheeky seagull decides to use his head as a perch! You can have fun with the bird's expression.

Two simple shapes form the sailor's head and body.

Now add a cap and a short, straight arm. Short thin legs make an amusing contrast with the chunky body in baggy shorts.

Add a top to his cap, making it as wide as his head. Give his face a big nose and a protruding pair of ears.

Above the cap, draw the seagull's body and head separately, leaving space for its legs and neck.

A big mustache and tousled hair give our sea-dog a nautical look.

Draw the mooring post, positioning its top just above the bottom of the sailor's shorts.

CARICATURES

Finish the face and tufty hair. Make the eyes glare up at the gull. You don't need to draw a mouth — the droopy mustache covers it, and also supplies its expression!

The curve of the gull's beak, and its upturned eye, give it a comically knowing look.

Draw in the mooring rope, crossing it with slanted lines to give it a twisted look.

A striped T-shirt is standard wear for cartoon sailors. An anchor on the cap badge is also essential!

Shape the feet, drawing one sideways on and the other turned toward us.

Why do seagulls fly across the ocean?

They don't want to get their feet wet!

The front of this foot looks wide because it is turned to us. Draw in broad, stubby toes.

Bouncing Baby

A baby isn't just a miniature adult. It's a completely different shape - rounded, with large head, small body, and short limbs. This roundness lends itself well to a cartoon approach — just think circles and you're halfway there!

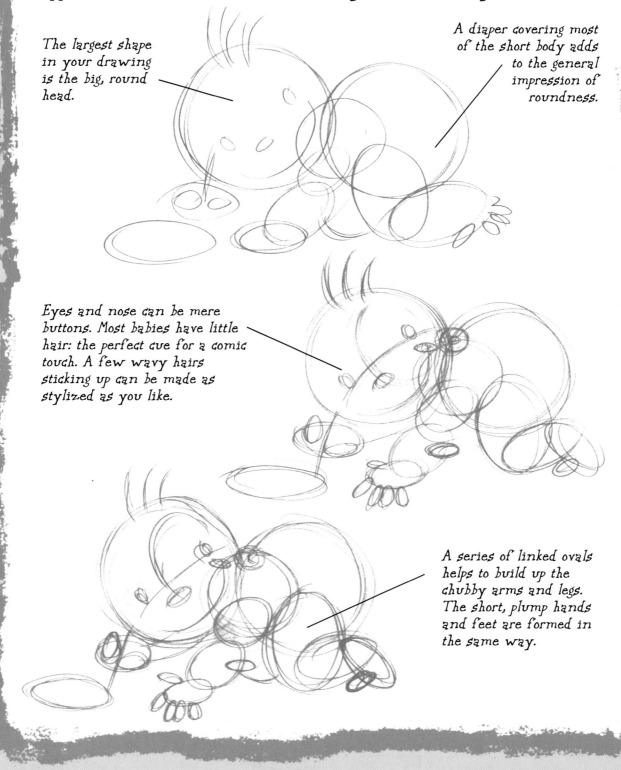

The largest shape in your drawing is the big, round head.

A diaper covering most of the short body adds to the general impression of roundness.

Eyes and nose can be mere buttons. Most babies have little hair: the perfect cue for a comic touch. A few wavy hairs sticking up can be made as stylized as you like.

A series of linked ovals helps to build up the chubby arms and legs. The short, plump hands and feet are formed in the same way.

Draw a little tongue peeping out as a mark of concentration, and add a dimple at the corner of the mouth.

You can suggest the texture of the diaper with little spikes and dashes.

Small children draw very simple faces. The joke here is that the baby's drawing looks very much like his own face.

As you complete your outlines, you can smooth out the links between the ovals of your original sketch.

Babies' toes are more flexible than adults'. Here the big toe is braced against the others for balance.

My little sister entered an art competition.

Did she win?

No, it was a draw.

Baby Driver

A baby seated in a toy car sounds quite a complicated drawing. But you can build it up in stages using easy shapes. By drawing the baby driver as simply as possible, you can focus attention on the toy car.

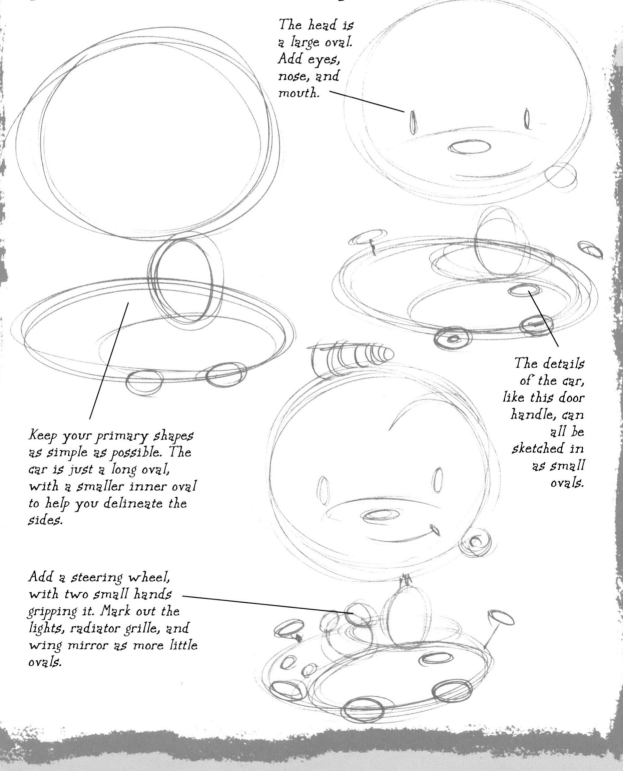

The head is a large oval. Add eyes, nose, and mouth.

The details of the car, like this door handle, can all be sketched in as small ovals.

Keep your primary shapes as simple as possible. The car is just a long oval, with a smaller inner oval to help you delineate the sides.

Add a steering wheel, with two small hands gripping it. Mark out the lights, radiator grille, and wing mirror as more little ovals.

Add a little flick of hair on top. The way it sticks up on top of the huge round head adds to the comic effect.

Eyes can be drawn as thin slits like this.

A single eyebrow is all you need to create an expression of surprised pleasure.

Save all the detail for the car, with its hood, door, and trimmings.

Ink in your outlines.

A white highlight at either end of the car helps to make it look shiny and new.

Happy Harriet

We've all met her — the little girl with too much bounce, always sure everyone is delighted to see her. Now you can draw her! Free, sweeping lines suggest her energy, and we all know what that huge grin means!

A curving line across the head helps you to place the enormous grin.

Block in the body between the legs, using a couple of ovals to establish the curved hems of jacket and skirt.

Use great big blobs for the feet — all the better to bounce on!

Add eyes and nose, and sketch in the grinning mouth. A shock of hair frames the face in a wide, umbrella-like shape.

Outstretched arms rarely stick straight out on either side, except in young children's drawings. By basing the arms on a curved line, you give them a more natural shape.

A collar and three buttons complete the jacket.

One foot is still in mid-air — Harriet is far too bouncy to stop moving while her picture is drawn!

Draw in the wrinkles of socks collapsing toward her ankles.

Even her hair looks energetic as a result of this bold, zig-zag outline.

Draw the top teeth and tongue within the smiling mouth.

Don't forget to add little highlights to add sparkle to the eyes.

Simon the Skateboarder

Scooting along on a skateboard
demands a great sense of balance.
You can't show this in a drawing
just by showing the skateboarder
standing upright. But curving the
body one way and the legs another
captures a sense of dynamism.

Set the large feet at
different angles on
the board.

This large oval will
form the head.

Sketch in the
face, setting the
eyes about
halfway down.

Make the body short
and distinctly curved
to lean backward.

Now you can draw the T-shirt.
Keep the arms and legs curved,
without sharp angles at knees
and ankles, to maintain a
feeling of flowing movement.

The skateboard
is easy to draw
— just a large
ellipse with
oval wheels.

Add a curve behind the head for hair, with an oval on top for the fringe.

This leg looks shorter because it is further away from us – and bent at the knee.

The T-shirt juts out at the back beyond the legs.

Rub out your guidelines and carefully ink in the outlines.

His fingers are crossed – and who can blame him!

Adding shadows beneath his feet makes the board look more solid, while the bold shading on the clothes makes the drawing look really modern.

Bouncing Billy

Bouncing on a giant spacehopper is great fun — but how do you get off? The humor in this cartoon lies in the boy's worried expression. It has just occurred to him that he is stuck, and sooner or later he is going to have to take a tumble.

This leg curves over the top of the ball.

The whole drawing is built up of rounded shapes.

Complete the head shape with another interlocking circle.

The lower leg curves roughly across the center of the spacehopper.

Now you can start outlining arms and legs. Remember to use curves rather than straight lines.

Draw in the face, with a small, worried mouth and little button eyes.

The hands are rounded, gripping the two handles.

This shoe is seen from underneath, so concentrate on the thick sole — most of the upper is hidden.

A wavy outline gives short, curly hair.

The body leans back in apprehension — how do I get off this thing?

Bob's Balloon

Draw the balloon as a long oval.

Short curved lines form arms, legs, and body.

Here we have Bob, taking his balloon for a walk. Perhaps he is coming home from a party — he certainly looks happy enough. Flying a balloon is a simple pleasure: keep your drawing simple to match.

Make the head a slightly flattened circle.

Hair doesn't have to be realistically drawn — have some fun with it!

A huge beaming smile runs right across his face.

Draw in his pants as wide tubes, with deep cuffs.

Bob's sweater forms a simple bell shape above his legs.

Bob's thumb closes over the string. You've got to hold tight!

A simple patch pocket enlivens his jumper.

The balloon's string ends in a decorative curl.

Add a knot at the end of the balloon.

One foot is flat on the ground, the other raised in mid-step.

Skipping Sam

This good old playground game goes in and out of fashion, but there's always someone with a skipping rope. Skipping can be graceful, but perhaps not with huge trainers and a rope that's starting to collapse!

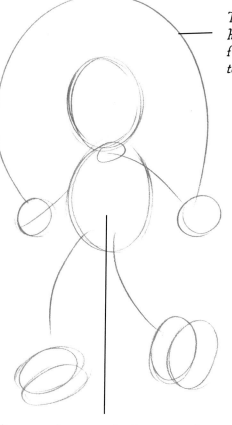

The rope curves high above the figure from hand to hand.

Mark out where the shorts end, halfway down the legs, with small ovals.

Start with a simple figure made up of circles and ovals, linked by curved lines for arms and legs.

Sketch in the baseball cap, hair, and a happy smile.

Sketching two overlapping ovals for each shoe will help you fit in the thick soles.

Add detail to the T-shirt and shorts, bending the body and legs backward to show movement.

Draw in the hands, gripping the rope's handles.

Establish the curve of the rope, and add a couple of kinks to the ends.

Short, skinny legs appear between shorts and sneakers.

Don't skip the task of rubbing out unwanted guidelines! You can make your cartoon as bright as you want.

Soccer Crazy

Soccer players twist themselves into some astonishing positions when trying to reach the ball. You hardly need to exaggerate these at all for a great cartoon. Here we have a player who is falling over backward in the attempt!

Draw a circle for the head. A short curve across the lower third marks out where the face broadens below the eyes.

Sketch in the arms along your guideline, and add a circle for the football just in front of a hand.

Body and leg form a single curve, from which the second leg stretches upward.

Add eyes and nose, and a small oval to mark out the ear.

Don't be afraid of rubbing out guidelines and drawing them again until you start to get the correct shapes.

Draw the hand with outspread fingers and thumb.

Small ovals mark out the legs of his shorts, at about knee level.

When you are happy with your rough sketch, finish drawing the face and arms. Your guidelines show you where the T-shirt ends and the shorts begin.

A lopsided grin can be very expressive. Cartoon faces usually don't look realistic because certain features are exaggerated to make them funny.

Thin, bendy arms without angular joints are flung out for balance.

Socks are more interesting to draw when they are falling down! A couple of curving lines form wrinkles.

What did the TV commentator shout when Dracula took a successful penalty?

'It's a ghoul!'

Baby Dinosaur

When we think of dinosaurs, we expect them to be huge and probably fierce. So let's do something quite different! This drawing turns our expectations on their heads by showing a cute baby, who is using his broken eggshell for a cot.

A circle with a slice off the top forms half an eggshell.

Above it, add a slightly slanted egg shape for a head.

Add guidelines for eyes and mouth.

. . . and draw a pair of claws clinging to the edge.

Give the shell a jagged edge, but leave this bit smooth . . .

Add more zig-zag edges behind the claws.

Big eyes and tiny teeth make the hatchling look babyish. You can make him look friendlier by adding speed marks round the tail so it seems to be wagging a puppy-like greeting.

Rub out this guideline when you have finished drawing the claws.

We don't know what dinosaur nests looked like, but sketching in a pile of twigs makes it clear that this egg is in a nest.

Caveman

Cavemen in cartoons always wear animal skins and carry huge stone clubs — it's a 'uniform' by which we recognize them. We don't expect them to look either wimpy or intellectual. You need to be strong to drag a woolly mammoth back home!

A big circle forms the thick body.

Place the short, broad head well down the body.

Long hair flowing outward helps to merge the head shape into the body, giving a bulky, squat look.

Draw the huge clubhead just overlapping the base of the body.

A simple curve forms heavy, frowning eyebrows.

Place the big, round hands about two thirds of the way down the body.

Give the club a tapering handle.

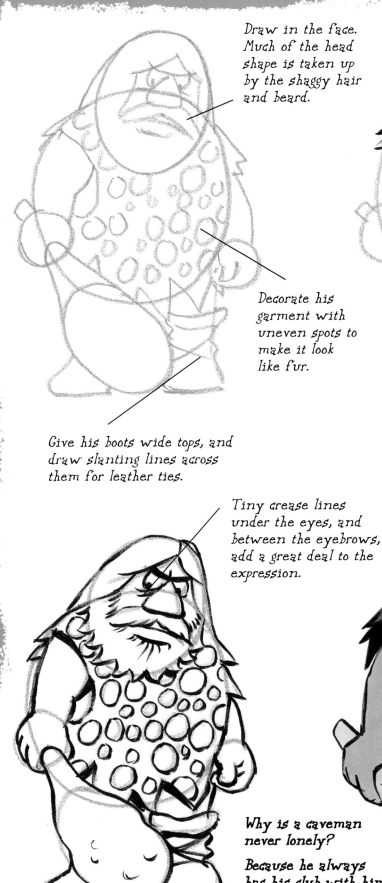

Draw in the face. Much of the head shape is taken up by the shaggy hair and beard.

Decorate his garment with uneven spots to make it look like fur.

Give his boots wide tops, and draw slanting lines across them for leather ties.

Finish the lower edge of his garment with a bold zig-zag edge — cavemen hadn't invented straight hems yet!

Tiny crease lines under the eyes, and between the eyebrows, add a great deal to the expression.

Why is a caveman never lonely?

Because he always has his club with him!

Woolly Mammoth

One inspiration for cartoons is having fun with names. We all know that the woolly mammoth gets his name from his shaggy coat. But why not draw him wearing a winter woolly? Back in the Ice Age, he would probably have welcomed it!

Start off with two rough balls — like a snowman.

Shape the hem of the sweater, and add a couple of short, chunky arms.

This arm ends in a curve, like a fin, to give the blunt shape of an elephant-like forefoot.

Sketch in the outlines of a woolly hat to match his sweater.

Draw in the huge, leaf-shaped ears on either side of the head.

The trunk is essential to identify the mammoth.

The tusk fits into a rounded socket.

The eyes are circles with their bases cut off by curves below. These curves help to make the face look chubby rather than flat. The rounded tusk socket helps, too.

A few wavy lines form toenails on the big, rounded feet.

Create a knitted texture for hat and sweater with rows of wiggly lines.

The trouble with knitting a sweater for one of these creatures is that you need a mammoth supply of wool!

Out of the Frying Pan...

The unexpected is always an amusing subject to draw. Here our caveman is running away from a ridiculously huge dinosaur, represented only by its foot. But the cave where he wants to hide isn't quite what he thinks it is!

Draw in the cliff just in front of the dinosaur.

Join the dinosaur's head to its body with a slim, curved neck, and shape the lower part of the body.

Start off your dinosaur with two ovals. The head is what matters in this picture, so make it huge.

The running dinosaur's foot is easily sketched within this rectangle.

Sketch in the caveman with this 'snowball' head and body.

The running man's head is turned right over his shoulder to look at the monster chasing him. He should look where he's going. Or should he?

Fringe the open jaws with lots of sharp teeth. The eye is set well back on the head. Small creases running from the inner edge of the eye give it more of a glare.

What do you call a one-eyed dinosaur?

D'youthinkesaurus.

And what do you call his dog?

D'youthinkesaurus Rex.

Small arms and dainty claws make a comic contrast with the dinosaur's huge head. But they are also based on real life — giant meat-eating dinosaurs ran on their hindlegs and had tiny 'arms.'

Saber-toothed Tiger

With animal cartoons, ask yourself what is the most obvious feature of your chosen animal. Then imagine what you can do with it. With the Saber-toothed Tiger, obviously it's his teeth. And, of course, he needs to keep them sharp . . .

Start with these three shapes — a head and two sections of body.

Two small circles on the head form ears, and a slightly larger one makes a paw. The other paw is set some distance away from and just below the head.

The shield-shaped nose is set high up, because the head is tipped back.

Draw a long shape for the file, running from one paw almost to the other. Leave a space for the handle.

Shape the feet and haunches, and add a curving tail ending in a large tassel.

Draw in the two saber teeth.

Short 'spin' marks show the movement of the file across the edge of the tooth.

Curl the toes of the forepaw round the file handle.

Spiky whiskers show on the left, but are mere dots on the other side of the face.

Make the stripes on the body uneven to match a tiger's markings. The tail is evenly banded, like a snake.

Dive Bomber

The inventive cartoonist can put dinosaurs to all sorts of uses. Here we have a pterodactyl standing in for an airplane. Try developing this idea: maybe you could use a long-necked swimming dinosaur as a Stone Age submarine.

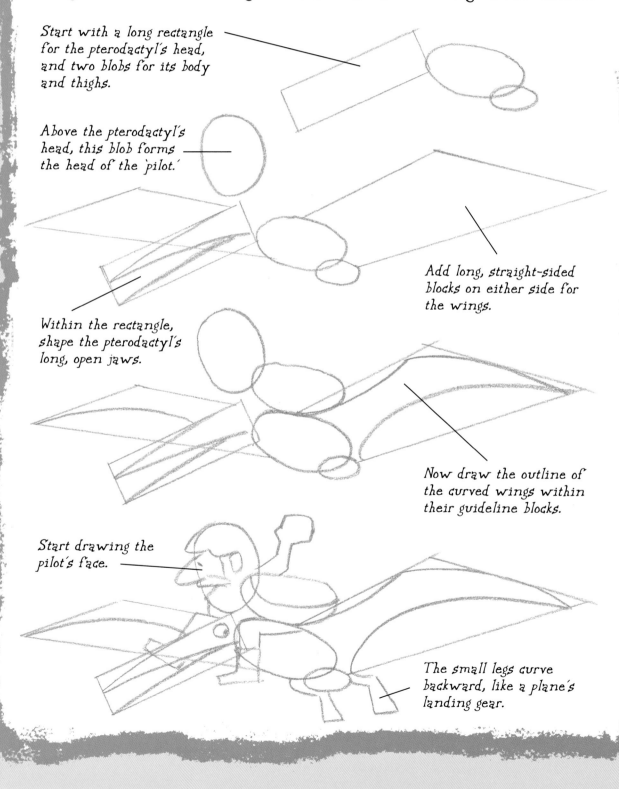

Start with a long rectangle for the pterodactyl's head, and two blobs for its body and thighs.

Above the pterodactyl's head, this blob forms the head of the 'pilot.'

Add long, straight-sided blocks on either side for the wings.

Within the rectangle, shape the pterodactyl's long, open jaws.

Now draw the outline of the curved wings within their guideline blocks.

Start drawing the pilot's face.

The small legs curve backward, like a plane's landing gear.

Add a small curved claw on top of each wing.

Within the outline of the pilot's shoulder bag, draw in his supply of rock 'bombs.'

The pilot's right arm curves forward across the wing.

Start turning the outline of his feet into a pair of boots.

His left hand holds the next stone 'bomb' raised ready to throw.

Roughen the edges of your original oval guideline for the pterodactyl's body. Now it looks like a furry chest, contrasting with the leathery wings.

Near the pterodactyl's head, draw the 'bomb' the pilot has just thrown right-handed, and add speed marks by his right hand to show the movement.

Artist

It's easy for you to sit down to draw. You have a table and chair to sit on, and pencils and paper are easy to buy. But what about the Stone Age artist? He had stone to sit on, and stone to paint on, but what did he use for a brush?

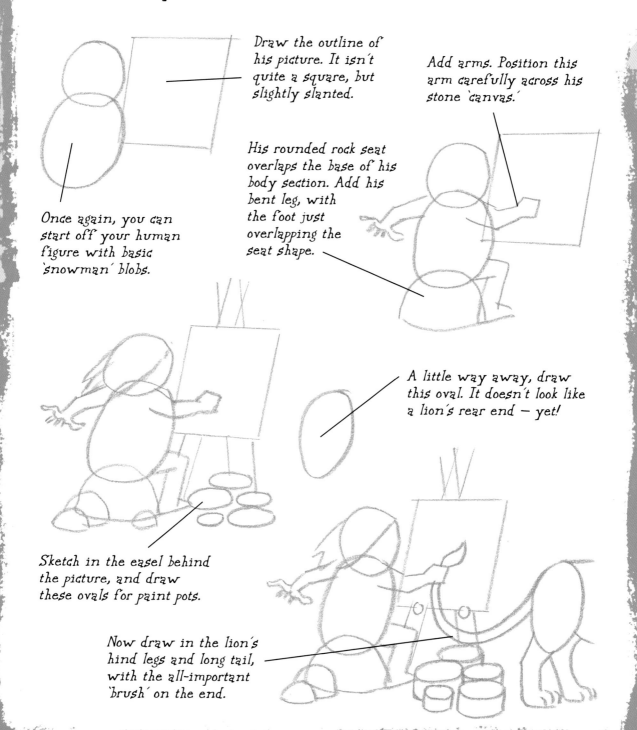

Draw the outline of his picture. It isn't quite a square, but slightly slanted.

Add arms. Position this arm carefully across his stone 'canvas.'

His rounded rock seat overlaps the base of his body section. Add his bent leg, with the foot just overlapping the seat shape.

Once again, you can start off your human figure with basic 'snowman' blobs.

A little way away, draw this oval. It doesn't look like a lion's rear end — yet!

Sketch in the easel behind the picture, and draw these ovals for paint pots.

Now draw in the lion's hind legs and long tail, with the all-important 'brush' on the end.

Sketch in the painting that the artist is producing with his unusual brush.

Finish drawing the crude easel — two pieces of wood secured at the top with twine. Make it look thick and solid enough to support a stone 'canvas.'

Complete the paint pots. Make them look chunky, because they are carved out of stone. Cartoon paint pots always have paint spilling messily over the lip. Perhaps yours do too!

You don't need the whole lion to tell the story — just his hindquarters will do.

Draw in the artist's traditional fur garment, giving it a jagged hem and a pattern of spots.

My brother's a terrible artist. He can't even draw the curtains!

Sunday Lunch

Stone Age man lived by hunting animals and gathering plants. What did he hunt? Well, in the cartoon Stone Age he simply has to hunt dinosaurs. The humor in this picture depends on the contrast between the tiny hunter and his huge catch.

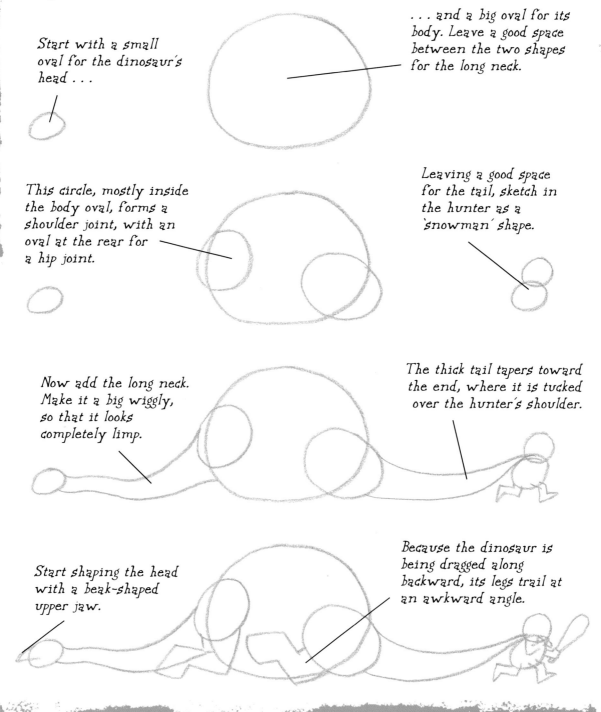

Start with a small oval for the dinosaur's head . . .

. . . and a big oval for its body. Leave a good space between the two shapes for the long neck.

This circle, mostly inside the body oval, forms a shoulder joint, with an oval at the rear for a hip joint.

Leaving a good space for the tail, sketch in the hunter as a 'snowman' shape.

Now add the long neck. Make it a big wiggly, so that it looks completely limp.

The thick tail tapers toward the end, where it is tucked over the hunter's shoulder.

Start shaping the head with a beak-shaped upper jaw.

Because the dinosaur is being dragged along backward, its legs trail at an awkward angle.